Physical Characteristics of the Japanese Tosa

(from the Fédération Cynologique Internationale's breed standard)

Back: Level and straight.

Croup: Slightly arched at the top.

Tail: Thick at the root, tapering towards the tip, reaching the hocks when let down.

Hindquarters: Muscles very developed, joints of stifle and hock moderately angulated, strong.

Belly: Well drawn up.

Coat: Short, hard and dense.

Color: Red, fawn, apricot, black, brindle. Slight white markings on chest and feet are permitted.

Feet: Tightly closed. Pads thick and elastic. Nails hard and preferably dark in color.

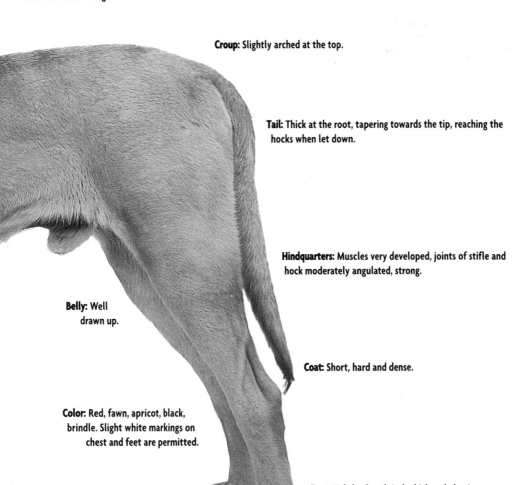

APR - 4

Japanese Tosa

By Steve Ostuni and DogStar Kennels

Contents

Training Your Japanese Tosa   **89**

By Charlotte Schwartz
Be informed about the importance of training your Japanese Tosa from the basics of housebreaking and understanding the development of a young dog to executing obedience commands (sit, stay, down, etc.).

Health Care of Your Japanese Tosa   **113**

Discover how to select a qualified vet and care for your dog at all stages of life. Topics include vaccinations, skin problems, dealing with external and internal parasites and common medical and behavioral conditions.

Behavior of Your Japanese Tosa   **142**

Learn to recognize and handle behavioral problems that may arise with your Japanese Tosa. Topics discussed include separation anxiety, aggression, barking, chewing, digging, begging, jumping up, etc.

KENNEL CLUB BOOKS: **JAPANESE TOSA**
ISBN: 1-59378-336-1

Copyright © 2003   Kennel Club Books, Inc.
308 Main Street, Allenhurst, NJ 07711 USA
Cover Design Patented: US 6,435,559 B2 • Printed in South Korea

Photographs by Isabelle Français, Carol Ann Johnson and Alice van Kempen with additional photographs by:

Norvia Behling, T. J. Calhoun, Carolina Biological Supply, David Dalton, Doskocil, James Hayden-Yoav, James R. Hayden, RBP, Bill Jonas, Dwight R. Kuhn, Dr. Dennis Kunkel, Mikki Pet Products, Phototake, Jean Claude Revy and Dr. Andrew Spielman.

Illustrations by Patricia Peters and Walter Hunt.

The publisher wishes to acknowledge the following owners and photographers:
Rick Babineau, Serena Burnett, Whitney Crockett, Donna Davis, Terry L. Edinger, Takashi Hirose, Walter W. Hunt, Michelle Jones, Bernd Leikhauf, Claudia Naber, Steve Ostuni, Julia Neiman, Anthony Recchia, Mariella Sachs, Anthony Smith, Mary A. Sullivan, Christine Tippelmann and Sanda Thompson.

The Japanese people have had the Tosa-inu (*inu* meaning "dog") as a part of their cultural heritage for more than 900 years. This Tosa has just won his championship in Japan and is adorned with the ornaments of a champion.

BACKGROUND AND HISTORY IN JAPAN

The Japanese Tosa-token, more commonly called the Tosa-inu or Tosa-ken, has been revered and feared throughout Japan for more than 900 years. The Japanese people consider the Tosa to be a Natural Treasure and, even with the breed's current popularity in the West, Tosas are rarely exported. The breed has also been referred to as the Japanese Mastiff or the Japanese Fighting Dog, but the Japanese Kennel Club (JKC) sanctions neither name. The name Japanese Fighting Dog seems to be a more generic term that has been used throughout time to refer to whatever was the predominant Japanese fighting breed of a given time period. It has been used in the past to describe the Akita but is now mainly used in reference to the Tosa.

Many Japanese breeds were named after the province in which they originated. The Tosa is the indigenous dog of Tosa-Wan (Tosa Bay), located in Kochi Prefecture on the southern Japanese island of Shikoku. Some older sources refer to the Tosa as

BRAIN AND BRAWN

Since dogs have been inbred for centuries, their physical and mental characteristics are constantly being changed to suit man's desires for hunting, retrieving, scenting, guarding and warming their masters' laps. During the past 150 years, dogs have been judged according to physical characteristics as well as functional abilities. Few breeds can boast a genuine balance between physique, working ability and temperament.

the Kochi-inu, which translates as "Kochi dog." The names Kochi-inu and Tosa-inu both refer to the same dog; however, Kochi-inu is no longer used to refer to the breed.

Known for its tenacious fighting ability and its extreme courage, the Tosa is unequaled among all canine species. The Tosa's athletic abilities are evenly balanced by its loyalty and devotion to home and family.

Although the Tosa we recognize today has a predominantly mastiff-like appearance, the original Tosa from Tosa-Wan is of spitz lineage with a shaggy coat, erect ears and a tail that curles over the hindquarters, similar to the modern Akita and Shiba-inu. These lupoid (wolf-like) canines were and still are common throughout Japan.

The tales of the Tosa date from the 11th century and are wrapped in the lore of Japan and, more specifically, Kochi Prefecture. The dogs were known as warrior companions and were used extensively in dog-fighting arenas. It has been said that the Tosa's stoicism, bravery and quiet approach to impending combat were presented as a training regimen for young Samurai warriors in order for them to learn the true meaning of courage in combat.

Dog fighting has been a long-standing tradition in Japan (as well as in many other countries around the world, including England and the US). There is a negative opinion of dog fighting in Western culture due to literature such as Jack London's *Call of the Wild* and Hollywood movies that depict the cruelties of the sport in the West. However, dog fighting in Japan is completely unlike the Western-style pit fights. This account from Jefferick Stocklassa, cited in *Molosser Magazine* (March 1985), offers a clear description of a Tosa match in Japan: "The Tosa fights are not allowed to be bloodthirsty. But the dogs wrestle and shake each other. Hence they do bite, but not to wound or kill the other, but to hold him and throw him down. Fights are immediately stopped when wounds are visible. A vet is always present. Furthermore, fights are carried out in public places, not secretly like with Pit Bulls."

The rules of Tosa combat are the same as those of Sumo wrestling. The objective is to pin or dominate an opponent. Most matches end in disqualification when referees and handlers, who are ever-present in the ring, separate combatants. Fights may be stopped when one dog whimpers, cowers or shows any sign of submission. A growl, a bark, a snarl or a cower is also grounds for disqualification. Noises of any kind are discouraged; hence, the Tosa is a very quiet dog.

GENUS *CANIS*
Dogs and wolves are members of the genus *Canis*. Wolves are known scientifically as *Canis lupus* while dogs are known as *Canis domesticus*. Dogs and wolves are known to interbreed. The term "canine" derives from the Latin-derived word "*Canis.*" The term "dog" has no scientific basis but has been used for thousands of years. The origin of the word "dog" has never been authoritatively ascertained.

Males are the only dogs that legally can compete in the ring. Bitches are strictly for breeding; however, they are fought or "rolled" at least once, sometimes more, in order to determine their instincts and abilities as fighting dogs. Characteristics such as viciousness, timidity or an unwillingness to engage in combat are considered disqualifications and would render such a bitch unsuitable for breeding.

Fighting Tosa dogs, especially champions, are very valuable. They are never fought to the death and are rarely seriously wounded. A winning Tosa can commonly be valued at six figures or more, very similar to a thoroughbred racehorse. There was a time when a Tosa may have provided the sole

Two Japanese champions! A champion Tosa and a champion Sumo wrestler.

whose dog of choice was the Kochi-inu (Tosa), eager to engage and compete in the ring with the Western dogs.

These Tosas, lupoid in appearance, were known throughout Japan as the most tenacious and capable of all Japanese fighting dogs. However, they rarely reached the weight of 50 lb (23 kg), while their Western counterparts often ranged from 100 to 150 lb (46 to 69 kg), sometimes even larger. Modern English Mastiffs can, and commonly do, weigh up to 250 lb (almost 115 kg). Unable to compete on equal terms due to their vast weight and size differences, some of the dog breeders/ fighters from Tosa-Wan decided to modify their breed. The first known crossbreeding was between an original Tosa (spitz-style) dog and an old-style Bulldog. It is said that the resulting puppies became the forefathers of our modern-day Tosa.

From this early modification came admixtures of Bulldog, Bloodhound, Mastiff, Great Dane, St. Bernard, Bull Terrier and Pointer. The results of these admixtures are the foundation of the Tosa we know today, and are obvious and easily recognized even by the most inexperienced of dog fanciers.

Each breed modification and/or improvement had a rhyme and a reason to it. Each compo-

source of income for a family, and the family's time was devoted to training and exercising their dog. The dog gained value and a family gained material wealth as a Tosa rose in standing through successful fights.

Dog fighting played a critical role in the development of the modern Tosa. Until the 1800s, Japanese breeds were virtually unknown outside the country; however, within Japan, fierce competition existed in the dog-fighting rings. In 1854, the Tokogawa government of Japan repealed its national isolation policy and opened trading with Western foreigners. When Western merchants came to Japan, they found the Samurai warrior clans,

nent breed was chosen for a specific purpose. The St. Bernard and Mastiff were introduced for size and strength, the Bulldog and Bull Terrier for tenacity and the Pointer for the concentration it takes to maintain focus. The Bloodhound added the extra skin whereby one dog can bite and the opponent still has the freedom and ability to turn around and bite back. The Doberman added intelligence and the Dogue de Bordeaux added bulk. The Great Dane contributed height, though the authors feel that it is debatable whether the added height actually increased performance ability, though it is attractive.

The dog breeders/fighters in Japan prefer a dog of light- to middle-weight proportions. The heavier dogs (150–200 lb) are more often used to attract tourists into the fighting arenas or are pictured in photos dressed in costly silk and gold-embroidered robes called *Miswashi*. Miswashi are custom-made to celebrate a Tosa's championship and usually show the owner's crest or coat-of-arms and the dog's name. While traveling in Japan, Western breeders have tried to purchase these robes for display; although never offered for sale, the cost would be astronomical for a full set. They are truly magnificent.

A Japanese champion Tosa winning in Kochi, Japan and wearing the ceremonial robes of a champion Tosa.

From the time of the cross-breedings, dog fighting became even more popular and large tournaments were held often throughout Japan. The early arenas were constructed of bamboo and were easily moved from one site to another. Tournaments were staged in public parks and Shinto shrines. Tosa dogs were led into the gazebo-style ring dressed in their custom Miswashi. Dog fighting maintained its popularity as a

Takashi Hirose, his mother and a Tosa champion, pictured in Japan in this historically significant photo.

THE JAPANESE MASTIFF

The Tosa may be referred to as the Japanese Mastiff. Many countries have a distinct mastiff breed: the Rottweiler of Germany; the Mastiff of Great Britain; the Dogue de Bordeaux of France; the Neapolitan Mastiff of Italy and the St. Bernard of Switzerland, just to name a few.

spectator sport until the years of World War II. With all available resources then devoted to the war effort, Tosas became a drain on the food and resources of Japanese society. At that point, the fighting and rearing of Tosa dogs were forbidden, some say punishable by death.

During those turbulent years, some of the most dedicated Tosa breeders took what may have been the last remaining handful of Tosa breeding stock and clandestinely hid the dogs in the mountainous areas surrounding Kochi Prefecture. After Japan surrendered to Western forces and the reconstruction of Japanese cities and society began, so also began the normalization that brought Japanese traditions back into the day-to-day lives of the Japanese people.

Tosa dog fighting, however, never regained its early popularity as a spectator sport and became instead an underground activity controlled by the Yakuza (Japan-

Ceremonial garb Miswashi worn by Tosa champions.

ese Mafia groups). Mainstream society turned a blind eye to the Tosa and its importance as a culturally and historically significant Japanese breed. The popularity and interest in Tosa dog fighting had waned, but the legality of the sport remained intact. Dog fighting maintained its legal status until recent years, when animal rights activists petitioned the Japanese Kennel Club as well as the Japanese government. They finally received favorable legisla-

tion that made dog fighting illegal throughout Japan except in Tosa-Wan (Kochi Prefecture).

This exemption was due to the fact that the Tosa is still considered a cultural icon. This status allows the people of Tosa-Wan to maintain strictly controlled fighting arenas where Japanese enthusiasts as well as Western tourists can observe the Tosa dog in its element, doing what it has been bred to do: exhibit courage and bravery in the fighting ring.

The Akita, like the Tosa, is a fighting dog derived from Japan. The Akita possesses Nordic spitz-dog qualities like the original Tosa.

In recent years, the Tosa has been favored by many Europeans, including Dutch, German and Spanish enthusiasts, who have taken to the breed with much fervor.

A young Tosa, showing much promise. Notice the confident stance and the alert expression on this dog's face.

THE TOSA IN THE WEST

Western interest in this rare breed may well have saved the Tosa from obscurity and possible extinction. By the late 1970s, the Tosa had made its way to Europe and, in the early 1980s, the Tosa was imported to the continental United States. American author Dr. Carl Semencic introduced many Americans and Europeans to the Tosa breed in his three popular books that featured the Tosa (among other breeds): *The World of Fighting Dogs*, *Pit Bulls and Tenacious Guard Dogs* and *Gladiator Dogs*.

According to the January 1984 edition of *Molosser Magazine*, the first Tosa to be registered in Europe was probably a female, Fujimusumu, registered in 1976. A male named Tomitake was registered in 1977 and shortly thereafter became a World Champion at the 1977 World Dog Show. Swedish photographer Jefferick Stocklassa and his Japanese wife, Mizuko Sasaki, are on record as the breeders of the first European litter of Tosas, which was born in the late 1970s or early 1980s. By 1982, we know of two more European litters, one bred by the Stocklassas in Sweden and the other born in Germany.

Due to close ties between Japan and Hawaii, there were Tosas in Hawaii for many years prior to this time, although little is known about their history.

However, we do know that they were crossbred with the Poi Dog, the local dog of Hawaii, and were of smaller stature and looked similar to a Pit Bull. In the early 1980s, Masaru Hirose, a prominent breeder from Kochi Prefecture in Japan, gave a Tosa to the Governor of Hawaii. Mr. Hirose's son, Takashi Hirose, presented Mutsu, a very impressive Tosa with a decidedly mastiff-like appearance, to the Governor. Donald Lee, an avid Tosa enthusiast and president of the Tosa-ken Association of America (the first Tosa club outside Japan), became Mutsu's caretaker. Mutsu's lineage produced some magnificent Tosas, some of whom were eventually placed on the West Coast of the US.

Also in the early 1980s, in the southern US, co-author Steve

Banira and Bidanchi of Tomahimeden Kennels in Germany. This handsome duo came from the last litter to be whelped in Germany before the ban on the breed in that country.

Ostuni purchased his first breeding pair of Japanese imports through his good friend, Eiko Smith. Coincidentally, the American actor Jack Palance met Masaru Hirose while filming Tosas for an episode of the television show *Ripley's Believe It or Not*. Mr. Hirose gave Kuma and Miss Kochi, a breeding pair of Tosas, to Mr. Palance. In 1988, Jerri Hall, owner of a Mutsu daughter, introduced the Palances to DogStar Kennels. Kuma and Miss Kochi were left in the care of DogStar Kennels in southern California, and their offspring became part of a strong breeding program.

Within two years, Steve Ostuni and DogStar Kennels began to share bloodlines, as they found their dogs quite compatible in quality and size. Mariella Sachs and Oak Valley Kennels imported a pair of breeding Tosas from the Tokyo area. Fire Mountain Kennels, also in California, obtained Tosa offspring from these dogs and started another line of American-bred Tosas. Yoko and Michael Galli also brought some imports from Tokyo to California. By the early 1990s, there was an active network of Tosa breeders in the US with bridges built to Japanese and European breeders.

WORLD-WIDE ATTENTION FOR THE TOSA

It was a turbulent time in the dog world. By the mid-1980s, there

Despite the problems that the breed faces in certain European countries, including the UK, the Tosa enjoys recognition by the Fédération Cynologique Internationale and can be shown in most countries on the Continent.

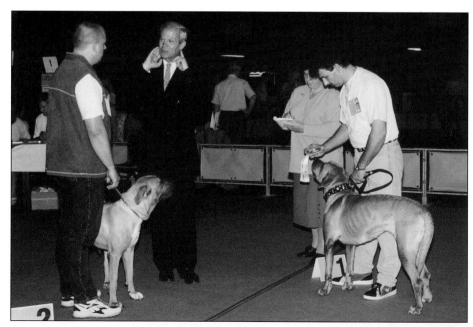

When properly bred, raised and trained, the Tosa can be a remarkable guard dog and companion. The breed is naturally blest with the brains and brawn to protect his family and property.

was an anti-Pit-Bull hysteria sweeping over America, and world-wide panic about fighting dogs increased to a feverish pitch. The Tosa was banned outright (and remains banned) in Great Britain, due only to public outcry and not because of any dangerous or harmful actions by a Tosa dog or a Tosa owner. Although there were fewer than 100 Tosas in the US, Tosa breeders and enthusiasts were diligent about public education campaigns to prevent damaging fictitious rumors about the Tosa from becoming accepted as fact.

Interest in the Tosa was very high. The breed was novel, extremely handsome and very expensive, as well as being a natural home and family protector. These factors put the Tosa at risk for overbreeding and subsequent loss of quality, physically and temperamentally. The International Tosa-ken Association was founded to provide information, guidance and education to both Tosa breeders and prospective Tosa owners. The organization had great success in uniting the Japanese, European and American breeders on behalf of the Tosa. The primary purpose was to inform the public about the Tosa breed and its enormous potential as a home and family guardian.

An interesting aspect in the Tosa's integration into the West is that the Japanese were not very anxious to export the breed. They were concerned that since the Tosa was a Natural Treasure and a cultural icon, it would be unwise to allow Western influence on the breed. They were very aware of the tendency of the Western breeders to alter breeds to fit "fashions" and to breed for size over function, a situation they saw with the Akita. Therefore, during the 1980s and 1990s, while there were cordial relations between Japanese and Western breeders, not many Tosas were exported from the main breeding centers in Japan.

However, Tosas from other areas in Japan and from Korea, Taiwan and other Asian countries were imported to Europe and America. These dogs were generally smaller in stature, with more of the Bulldog- and Doberman-type looks rather than the mastiff look of the dogs from Kochi Prefecture. The differences can still be seen, and they provide a significant variety within the breed today.

In the 1990s, the popularity of the Tosa continued to grow. Dedicated Western breeders invested the time, energy and money to import Tosas from Japan. Americans Serena Burnett of DogStar Kennels and Steve Ostuni traveled to Kochi Prefecture in 1993 to obtain additional breeding stock. They imported Ryoma, a 170-lb dark red male from the Hirose kennel. Steve Ostuni also took the first true black male to the US, obtained from Shiji Sasaki of Kochi, Japan. Ms. Burnett and Mr. Ostuni observed and studied the Tosa in its native element and forged strong ties with Tosa breeders in Japan.

These American breeders formed an alliance with the Tosa breeders/fighters in the Kochi area and determined a plan of action for the breed as a whole. Together, they petitioned the Japanese Kennel Club to upgrade and clarify breed standards and to legitimize the Tosa as a distinct breed. By focusing on Tosas' uses as family companions and guardians, they were taken out of the fighting arenas controlled by the Yakuza, the Japanese underground. The emphasis today is to utilize the natural instincts of the Tosa as a family and home guardian, to show them in the conformation and obedience rings, to train them as therapy dogs and to minimize the focus on dog fighting. With these objectives in place, Tosas are currently thriving in Japan and elsewhere throughout the world.

While doing research for this book, many Tosa breeders and owners world-wide were contacted for information. Two of the most complete histories of the Tosa came from Berndt Leikauf in Germany and R. Schol and M.

This Tosa is participating in the World Dog Show in Amsterdam, having placed first in her class.

Schrieken in the Netherlands. These histories are interconnected and both tell stories of enthusiasm and obstacles.

In Germany, interest in the Tosa began in 1975 with Hermann Heuser. A rare-breed enthusiast, he owned some of the more exotic breeds at the time. In his six-year quest to locate Tosas, he was told repeatedly by Japanese business-

men and the Japanese embassy that the Tosa was a legend and did not really exist. This was most likely due to the fact that dog fighting, and therefore the fighting breeds, including the Tosa, were out of favor in Japan and not known to the general public.

In 1981, a chance meeting with a Japanese businessman resulted in Heuser's receiving a gift of a breeding pair of Tosas imported from Japan. From this pair, 34 pups eventually were produced. Very few were shown in dog shows and only one was ever used for breeding. Heuser sold his breeding pair to Wolfgang Fink, who worked for years to bring new bloodlines into Germany to cross with these two original dogs. Fink imported a male from the Stocklassas in Sweden, but was never able to produce offspring. He tried to import from Donald Lee in

Hawaii, but the cost was prohibitive. Eventually Fink gave up breeding Tosas and, for a while, the breed seemed to die out in Germany.

In the meantime, Gerd Jessen fell in love with a little Tosa female from Heuser's last litter, but only succeeded in breeding one litter. One excellent-quality male, Akihito, resulted, but after several years of trying to find a suitable female to breed with him, the Jessens also gave up Tosa breeding.

In 1996, Berndt Leikauf worked with the Jessens to find a suitable female for Akihito. They imported a female from DogStar Kennels and other dogs from Fire Mountain Kennels, both in the US. By crossing these dogs with other Tosas from American and European kennels, they were successful in promoting a strong Tosa breeding line.

European countries were very hard-hit by the hysteria over fighting dogs in the 1980s and 1990s. The Tosa was banned outright in England and remains so today. France also has banned the Tosa and several other breeds. In Germany, until recently, the laws restricting ownership of several breeds, including the Tosa, were very strict and, in some districts, the dogs were taxed at 2000%. This was a devastating blow to the Tosa breeding program. In January 2001, the Tosa and 38 other breeds were banned. Breeding and importing these breeds were forbidden, so it is feared that the Tosa will once again become extinct in Germany. Some dedicated dog lovers are fighting these laws with some success, and they hope to work with other Tosa enthusiasts and dog lovers throughout the world in order to gain support and eventually reverse this ban.

The Netherlands' history began in the early 1980s with a Tosa imported from Germany. With great effort, two more Tosas were imported from Japan and, from these, the Netherlands' breeding program was started. The popularity of the breed was high, and there was little chance of importing anything from Japan, so the breeders were able to sell all of the dogs they produced. Lack of new bloodlines and 13 years of close breeding led to some temperamental and physical problems in the Tosas of that area.

In 1998, a fresh bloodline from DogStar Kennels in the US was introduced, which refreshed the bloodlines and brought in the more massive and powerful Tosa type that is so attractive. At this time, the Tosa breeders and owners in the Netherlands are working diligently to breed "healthy and typical Tosas," which they acknowledge "will not be possible without good imports." The breeding population is small, but, in their words, the "will to learn and to breed good Tosas is enormous."

Although the Tosa is not the dog for everyone, the breed is still gaining popularity worldwide. In Asian countries, especially Korea, Tosas are rarely used as pets, companions or guardians. There they still exist mainly as a fighting breed. In Europe, Canada, the United States and even parts of South America, the Tosa is well known and respected as a superior natural guard dog and is used exclusively as a family companion and home guardian. Tosa owners and breeders agree that there will be many years of endeavor ahead in order to preserve the Tosa-inu in accordance with Japanese standards as well as to ensure the proper balance of temperament, type and conformation in our favored breed, the Tosa.

CHARACTERISTICS OF THE

JAPANESE TOSA

The Japanese Tosa is a strong, muscular dog with a loyal and protective temperament. It makes an excellent home guardian and is an agile athlete, especially for its size and weight. The same characteristics that made the Tosa an excellent fighting dog have made it a good choice as a home guardian and working dog.

PHYSICAL CHARACTERISTICS

Since the Tosa is a mastiff, it should not be slight of build. The broad head possesses a wrinkled brow, which becomes more prominent when the dog is alert. As in most breeds, the female's head is not as broad as the male's and should appear more feminine. The Tosa has a strong jaw and its teeth form a scissors bite. The dark eyes (sometimes lighter in puppies) show an expression of dignity and loyalty. The rim of black around the eye absorbs sunlight and prevents the reflection of the sun's rays into the eyes.

With its somewhat pendulous, thick, black lips, the Tosa is sometimes mistaken for a hound breed at various stages of its life, but, as a mature dog, no one should make this mistake. The muzzle can be the same color as the dog's coat or can be black, with a black nose. The ears are shaped in a "V" and are considered a "drop" ear. The hair on the ears is the softest on the dog's body.

Another important physical characteristic that sets the Tosa

WRESTLING WITH A HEELER

Puppies' play reflects their instinctual nature. In one Tosa litter, the dam adopted an orphaned Australian Kelpie. During play, the Tosas would bite and hold onto one another, wrestling hard in the style of Japanese dog fighting. The Kelpie would nip at the sides and legs of the Tosa pups and then run, just like a herding dog would do to keep his flock in line. It was clear that both breeds were curious about and not entirely comfortable with the other's style of play. We enjoyed watching the puppies learn each other's styles until they were all using both techniques effectively.

TEMPERAMENT AND TRAINABILITY

The Tosa temperament is marked by patience, composure, boldness and courage. A Tosa with true molosser type should exhibit an impeccable strength of character. This guardian breed should alert the family when strangers are present, but can usually be socialized with strangers on its own property once introduced. Unless provoked, a Tosa should not show aggression towards strangers while away from his property. This characteristic is one of the most desirable traits of this breed because it leads to creating a safe, effective guard dog.

The Tosa has shown amazing tolerance, patience and adaptability to most family activities, and with children in general. Most Tosas accept children immediately, even if they have never been

apart from other breeds is its dewlap. Again, males have a more prominent dewlap, and it more closely resembles that of the Dogue de Bordeaux than the pendulous dewlap of the Neapolitan Mastiff. The high withers, level and straight back, slightly arched croup, deep broad chest and well-drawn-up belly gives the Tosa the appearance of a strong, muscular athlete.

The coat is short, with various levels of coarseness. Color ranges from fawn to red, black and brindle, with the fawn or red being the most preferred. Slight white markings on the chest and paws are most acceptable for this breed.

The Tosa is gentle and playful with children, although supervision is necessary with such a large, strong dog so that no unintentional mishaps occur.

CAUTION: LOW DROOL

It is the loose skin around the mouth that makes many mastiff breeds messy droolers. Tosas have tighter bottom lips than most other mastiffs and therefore can't compare with dogs like the Dogue de Bordeaux and the Neapolitan Mastiff in the slobber department.

required in any given situation.

Tosa males tend to show more aggression than females, especially towards other male dogs, although some females need to be watched around dogs they don't know. The Tosa will generally not challenge a dog of smaller size, but will most likely not back down when challenged. For this reason, females are usually easier to walk in public and in dog parks, where encounters with other dogs are most likely.

It is imperative that all Tosa owners properly socialize and train their Tosas at a young age. We have been very successful in curbing aggressiveness while keeping the spirit of the dog intact by being diligent in the training and socialization process. This is not a breed that needs a heavy hand with training, but will learn early on to listen to commands. Responsible ownership is the key to successfully living with a Tosa.

Like most dominant breeds, usually the down command is the hardest for the Tosa to accept readily. That's why teaching this at an early age is important. Food motivation is a great training tool as most Tosas are highly food-motivated. Owners will learn quickly about the necessity of teaching them to take the food gently. Tosa owners have also used clicker training with success and found that the Tosa exhibits a high level of intelligence and abil-

socialized with them. They seem to have a natural bond with children and were used as babysitters by the Japanese people. Because of the breed's high pain tolerance, the Tosa is ideal for the rough play of some children who like to sit on and may accidentally step on their Tosa friend. This breed is not reactive when surprised and seems to use its intelligent nature to evaluate the best behavior

ity to learn quickly in training sessions. Praise is also a good motivator in training this breed. The Tosa does not need constant repetition once a command is learned and does best when new things are constantly introduced.

As with the training of all animals, providing a good foundation and consistency in training is paramount. Many times, the owner needs more training than the dog, and the Tosa owner should be willing to make the commitment to learn with his animal and become a good and responsible handler. Obedience and handling classes are an excellent way to socialize your Tosa, while learning the skills you both need to have the best possible relationship. Sometimes the Tosa can be stubborn during training sessions, but this is not predominant characteristic of the breed. Patience during these times is the best approach to having the dog see it "your way."

The highly sensitive emotional nature of the Tosa is exhibited most often during training sessions. They do not like to be reprimanded and will look at their owners with the saddest eyes when given the slightest harsh word. This characteristic makes them very trainable both on- and especially off-leash, when tone of voice becomes an important tool.

Tosa owners have been

A BIG DOG IN A SMALL YARD
For a giant breed, the Tosa is unique in its ability to adapt to a small space. The average yard in Japan is 9 feet square and the average home is fairly small, so the Japanese bred a large dog that could do well in small spaces.

successful with this breed in obedience trials, conformation classes, ring sport, weight pulling and Schutzhund, and some Tosas have received their therapy dog titles. Because of their desire to please, they are adaptable to most situations and are not hesitant to try new things, especially when rewarded by praise.

THE TOSA IN THE HOME
The Tosa loves to be with his family and is an excellent and adaptable traveler. He usually lies quietly nearby when possible, but he likes to have his own space within the household. When outside, a Tosa sometimes will follow his owner from window to window as the owner moves about in the house, making himself comfortable while looking through the window until the owner moves to the next room. With that said, however, the Tosa is an independent breed and does well without the company of other dogs or human companions.

This breed is incredibly clean and many times can be found licking its paws and legs like a cat after a meal. A Tosa usually picks one spot in the yard, far away from intrusion and sometimes hidden, in which to relieve himself. When in a new environment, and especially when traveling, it usually takes the Tosa a while to feel comfortable in his new surroundings and find an

POSITIVE FIGHTING ATTRIBUTES
Some of the characteristics that make the Tosa such a fantastic family dog are directly related to its origins as a fighting dog. Loyalty to their owners is a prime characteristic of fighting breeds, and this is a predominant trait in the Tosa. High pain tolerance was prized in fighting dogs; this is beneficial around children, since a Tosa will not react out of pain if a child, in normal youthful exuberance, falls on the dog or pulls on a tail or ears. In the Tosa fighting ring, any sound made by the dog meant instant disqualification; Tosas have retained this trait and will usually only bark to sound an alert or warning. In Japan, the Tosa dogs mingle freely outside the fighting ring, but, once in the fighting ring, are fiercely aggressive. This is modified well in the family companion dog of today. The Tosa is relaxed and friendly when at the park or at the vet's office, but will guard your home and family protectively.

adequate toileting area.

Tosas also make great outdoor dogs when provided adequate shelter from the elements. They tend to be a quiet breed that generally only barks when necessary. They have been successfully socialized with a variety of animals, including horses, cats, birds and, of course, other dogs. Again, socialization at an early age with a variety of animals is important with this breed.

We usually don't suggest having two males or two females together, because the Tosa is a dominant breed. Some people have been successful with a Tosa living with a same-sex dog of a smaller size or a less dominant breed, but the other dog should be in the home prior to bringing in the Tosa puppy in order to make this situation really successful. Puppies will generally not challenge an older dog, and the respect gained as a puppy will carry forward into the later years of their relationship. Introduction of a Tosa puppy to a home with another dog should be done carefully and the reaction of the animals monitored. Make sure that, by bringing in a puppy, you are not upsetting the balance in the home to such a degree that conflict is imminent.

ACTIVITIES AND ABILITIES
Playtime, training and exercise with your Tosa puppy are times of great pleasure for both of you. Be sensitive to your pup—Tosa puppies are usually alert, full of energy and eager to interact. If your pup seems tired or reluctant to interact, give him time to relax. This helps protect his growing body from overexertion. Due to the rapid growth of your Tosa puppy, his tendons, ligaments and joints are under great stress.

Puppies need time to replenish their bodies and this, in turn, keeps their immune systems strong. Remember that your pup's immune system is most vulnerable from three to six months of age and that most of his growth takes place in the first year.

During any physical activity with your puppy, pace yourself and be alert to changes in your pup's demeanor that could signal fatigue. Training or play sessions should be limited to a few minutes at a time. When walking with your pup, start slowly and for short distances. Slowly increase the time and/or distance of these activities for the first few months. Puppies kept in small enclosures don't have a chance to strengthen their bodies with natural movements and we have found that this leads to more incidences of knee injuries in later life. Be

At 11 months of age, this Tosa from DogStar Kennels is adaptable, friendly with children and capable of protecting his family.

SONG OF THE TOSA

The Tosa has a distinctive song unlike any we've heard in any other breed. Tosas are the "bass-baritones" of the dog chorus. Their song consists of a series of sonorous, elongated, descending tones that sound like deeply placed "woo-woo-woo-woos." Some of their singing sounds like the deep drones often heard in Far Eastern chanting, in which many different pitches are produced at once in one long single line.

sure that your Tosa, both as a puppy and as an adult, has ample space to move freely.

Long-distance running is not advised for growing puppies. A healthy adult Tosa may be conditioned to long-distance running with careful training. With proper training, Tosas can walk 3–5 miles easily. Avoid strenuous exercise on hot days.

Tosas love to play, and tug-of-war or other physical activities delight them. They are not usually thrilled with games like fetch, but they love to chase a ball or frisbee... just don't expect them to bring it back to you! Give them old towels or rope toys to chew, and this will occupy them for hours. We don't suggest riding a bicycle with your

Tosa unless he is impeccably trained. It is too dangerous to have a 100-plus-pound dog who might swerve in front of you or run into the bicycle you are riding.

HEALTH CONCERNS

Tosas live for an average of 8–12 years, which is standard for most of the giant breeds. Like most large-boned dogs, hip dysplasia is the most common problem seen in the breed. Reputable breeders will have their Tosas screened for hip dysplasia prior to breeding. This practice helps to minimize but will not eliminate cases of dysplasia.

The problem has been compounded in recent years with the increased popularity of the Tosa breed. Novices and incompetent people have begun to breed and have usually not followed sound breeding practices including x-rays for dysplasia. As a result, there are more cases of dysplasia than need be. It is a constant battle for the reputable breeder to find and breed sound dogs and to produce sound puppies.

Bloat (torsion) is a big danger to Tosas and to all deep-chested breeds. In this often-fatal condition, the dog's stomach twists in the chest cavity, causing extreme distress and preventing blood flow to the organs. There has been much research done on the causes and prevention of bloat. Here are some of the most effective recommendations:

1) Feed your dog on an elevated surface at chest level—a comercially made bowl stand or even a homemade wooden box with a hole for the feeding dish works well;
2) Do not feed for at least one hour before or after heavy exercise;
3) Do not feed right after the dog has consumed a lot of water;
4) Do not leave the food out; collect it within 15–20 minutes whether or not it is finished (no free feeding);
5) Moisten dry kibble slightly so that it will expand in the bowl and not in your Tosa's stomach;
6) If your Tosa is greedy and eats quickly, reduce the air swallowed by putting something large and inedible in the food bowl so that the dog has to pick around the object and thus eat more slowly;
7) Know the symptoms of bloat; check your Tosa regularly for several hours after eating for signs like a bloated stomach, retching, gagging or noticeable discomfort;
8) Know the closest emergency vet and have a plan to get your dog there *immediately*. If caught early and treated rapidly, your Tosa may survive bloat and lead a normal life.

The stress of rapid growth on a Tosa's joints, tendons and ligaments can lead to cases of panosteitis and

TAKING CARE
Science is showing that as people take care of their pets, the pets are taking care of their owners. A recent study published in the *American Journal of Cardiology* found that having a pet can prolong his owner's life. Pet owners generally have lower blood pressure, and pets help their owners to relax and keep more physically fit. It was also found that pets help to keep the elderly connected to their communities

BEWARE THE STOIC

It is often hard to tell if a Tosa is sick because the breed is exceptionally stoical. It is as if they carry the fighting spirit from their background and will not give in to physical weakness. For this reason, pay close attention to your Tosa—he will not often be obvious about sickness or pain.

ruptured cruciate ligament (pulled knee). Panosteitis is more commonly knows as "growing pains." It looks like a vague or wandering lameness and is often accompanied by a slight fever. It usually goes away after a while, but be extra careful about exercise and other stressful activities during this time. Your vet may recommend children's aspirin and rest to help speed recovery.

With a ruptured ligament, your Tosa will limp on a hind leg or hold it off the ground altogether. With limited activity and nutritional supplements, the condition can sometimes heal itself. Your vet should try this approach before considering surgery to repair the ligament. Results from surgery are unpredictable, due in part to the large size of the dog and the extremely long recovery time. During the recovery time, activity is severely restricted and the whole process requires much patience and care from both you and your Tosa.

Other minor concerns include cherry eye, which is easily corrected by a simple surgery. Skin and ear infections are almost nonexistent. Lick sores are raw areas caused by excessive licking, usually on the paws or bottom part of the legs. It is most commonly believed that these result from discomfort due to joint or other skeletal problems. The exact source is hard to find; usually it is only possible to treat the symptoms.

When you are looking for a vet for your Tosa, find one who has experience with large dogs in general and hopefully giant breeds. It is critical that you have the best advice and the most up-to-date information about medical and alternative practices for your Tosa's health concerns. An experienced vet will be an invaluable ally for you and your dog.

HIP DYSPLASIA IN PURE-BRED DOGS

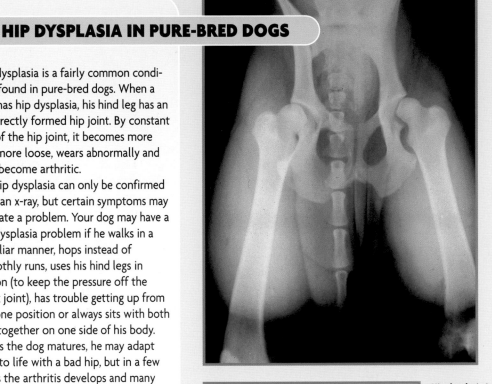

Hip dysplasia is a fairly common condition found in pure-bred dogs. When a dog has hip dysplasia, his hind leg has an incorrectly formed hip joint. By constant use of the hip joint, it becomes more and more loose, wears abnormally and may become arthritic.

Hip dysplasia can only be confirmed with an x-ray, but certain symptoms may indicate a problem. Your dog may have a hip dysplasia problem if he walks in a peculiar manner, hops instead of smoothly runs, uses his hind legs in unison (to keep the pressure off the weak joint), has trouble getting up from a prone position or always sits with both legs together on one side of his body.

As the dog matures, he may adapt well to life with a bad hip, but in a few years the arthritis develops and many dogs with hip dysplasia become crippled.

Hip dysplasia is considered an inherited disease and can usually be diagnosed when the dog is three to nine months old, though two years of age is the benchmark for a dog to be definitely cleared as dysplasia-free. Some experts claim that a special diet might help your puppy outgrow the bad hip, but the usual treatments are surgical. The removal of the pectineus muscle, the removal of the round part of the femur, reconstructing the pelvis and replacing the hip with an artificial one are all surgical interventions that are expensive, but they are usually very successful. Follow the advice of your veterinarian.

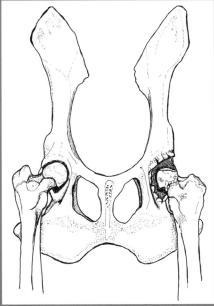

Hip dysplasia is a badly worn hip joint caused by improper fit of the bone into the socket. It is easily the most common hip problem in larger dogs, but dogs of any breed can be affected by hip dysplasia. The illustration shows a healthy hip joint on the left and an unhealthy hip joint on the right.

BREED STANDARD FOR THE

JAPANESE TOSA

The breed standard for any dog describes the ideal specimen of that breed. The standard is usually developed by the show-dog community and breeders to adequately set forth the desired characteristics of the breed. In the US, a breed's standard is written by the parent club and then approved by the American Kennel Club (AKC), although the AKC currently does not recognize the Tosa.

A conformation judge will use the breed standard of the hosting kennel club and compare the dogs in competition against the standard. A breeder will compare the offspring against the standard to choose which puppies are worthy of showing and breeding. Those puppies with minor flaws are usually sold as pets.

The Fédération Cynologique Internationale (FCI) breed standard for the Japanese Tosa is not complicated and it does not use exact measurements in describing the lengths and widths of the dog's various body parts like so many other breed standards do. We, therefore, sometimes see great variation within this breed, and the Tosa can by no means be considered a "cookie-cutter" breed. Many Tosa breeders and owners like this variation within the breed, which they feel makes each dog a true individual.

The variation in the breed can mostly likely be attributed to four factors: relative newness of the breed, different Tosa types, weight classifications and recent show-dog status.

1) *The relative newness of the breed:* The breed started its evolution in the late 1800s when the original Shikoku dog was bred with Western dogs. According to the breed standard, the introduction of new bloodlines was still ongoing in 1924 with the introduction of the Great Dane. There is speculation that the mixing of the Tosa with other breeds has occurred even more recently.

2) *The different Tosa types:* There are different types of Tosa dogs—the Mastiff-type, the Bullmastiff-type, the Pointer-type and the Doberman-type. The current standard is very close to the Mastiff-type Tosa.

3) *Weight classifications:* The Tosa was given fighting classifications of lightweight, middleweight and heavyweight.

4) *The recent show-dog status:* The Tosa was considered only as a fighting dog and family guardian until the mid-1980s, when it started to gain popularity as a show dog, mostly in the US and Europe.

There has been a push towards enhancing the FCI breed standard to further define the breed's characteristics; the Japanese Kennel Club has taken this under consideration. The potential Tosa owner can use the breed standard to compare puppies in a litter against each other, and to see if the sire and dam have the characteristics listed as important in the breed standard. The authors' notes are presented in italics.

FÉDÉRATION CYNOLOGIQUE INTERNATIONALE STANDARD FOR THE JAPANESE TOSA

ORIGIN
Japan.

UTILIZATION
Formerly fighting dog, nowadays watchdog.

FCI CLASSIFICATION
Group 2 Pinscher and Schnauzer type, Molossian type and Swiss Mountain and Cattle Dogs. Section 2.1 Molossian type. Mastiff type. Without working trial.

Judges use the breed standard to determine which dogs best conform to the description contained therein. This young Tosa bitch was selected as the best of her class at a show in Holland.

Profile showing a structurally sound, well-balanced Tosa, indicating substance and strength with athleticism and agility.

BRIEF HISTORICAL SUMMARY

Japan has a long history of dog fighting, beginning in the 14th century. With such a history in the background, this breed was produced as a hybrid of the Shikoku-ken and Western breeds. Named after the area where they were bred, these dogs are sometimes called "Japanese Mastiffs." The Western dogs used for creating the breed were Bulldogs (1872), Mastiffs (1874), German Pointers (1876) and Great Danes (1924), all of which were used to improve the breed by sequential mating. According to some accounts, St. Bernards and Bull Terriers were also involved, but it is not known in what years they were used. The Tosa's established features of stamina and the fighting instinct typically found in Mastiffs may be attributed by the involvement of such breeds.

According to the Japanese breeders, there are several types of Tosa due to the breeds used to create them—Mastiff-type, Bullmastiff-type, Pointer-type, Doberman-type. The current standard is very close to the Mastiff-type Tosa. Older Japanese Kennel Club (JKC) documents sometimes refer to the Tosa as the Japanese Mastiff; however, it was not the JKC's intention to promote the name Japanese Mastiff. When the Japanese compared the Mastiff to the Tosa, they considered the Mastiff shy and therefore not good for fighting. The Tosa is very smart, an aspect bred for by using the Doberman. The Great Dane also played an important role in creating the Tosa of today.

GENERAL APPEARANCE

Large-sized dog with a stately manner and robust build. The dog has hanging ears, short hair, a square muzzle and hanging tail thick at the root.

The Tosa is a slow-maturing dog. We find full maturity in an adult male at around the age of five years.

BEHAVIOR/TEMPERAMENT

The temperament is marked by patience, composure, boldness and courage.

Due to the nature of this breed as a guardian, Tosas should not exhibit shyness. Puppies should be socialized with people and other animals at a young age. Obedience training is very important, and Tosas should be started with basic obedience as puppies.

CRANIAL REGION

Skull: Broad.

The Tosa is considered to have a brachycephalic head—a short

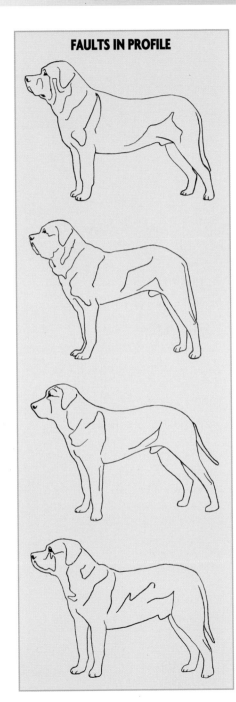

FAULTS IN PROFILE

Long body, low on leg, soft topline, weak rear.

Upright shoulders, weak pasterns, high in rear, lacking proper rear angulation, too straight.

Generally lacking substance, narrow front, toes out, upright shoulders, high in rear, lacking angulation in rear, soft topline.

Loaded shoulders, high in rear, weak rear, cowhocked, low on leg.

The ideal Tosa head.

skull that is wide between the cheekbones or zygomatic bones. *The Tosa has a wrinkled brow that gives it a slightly worried look. This wrinkle becomes more prominent when the dog is alert. Many Tosas also possess a characteristic wrinkle that falls from the outside corner of the eyelid straight down the cheek. The skull of the male Tosa is broader than that of the female. The female's head appears more feminine.*

Stop: Rather abrupt.
The stop is the angle between the bridge of the nose to the forehead. A deep stop allows for good frontal vision and is most developed in short-faced breeds.

FACIAL REGION
Nose: Large and black.

Muzzle: Moderately long. Nasal bridge straight.
The muzzle can be the same color as the dog's coat or black. The lips are thick and black and moderately pendulous. When viewed from the front, they form an inverted "V" or slightly pointed inverted "U" shape. This breed possesses hanging flews (corner rear portion of the upper lips).

JAWS
Upper and lower jaws strong.

TEETH
Strong with scissors bite.

EYES
Rather small, dark brown in color with dignified expression.
The eyes are round to slightly almond-shaped. A lighter eye in younger dogs is permissible but should darken with age. The eyes are rimmed in black. Dark rims tend to be preferred for most breeds as they absorb sunlight and do not reflect sunlight into the eyes.

Many wrinkled breeds suffer from entropion (eyelid rolled inward—inverted) and/or ectropion (eyelid turned outward—everted). These conditions can cause irritation and injury to the eye.

EARS
Relatively small, rather thin, set high on the skull sides, hanging close to the cheeks.

THE MYTH ABOUT LIGHT EYES

There is a Japanese myth about eye color preference in the Tosa. The dark eye in the Tosa is important to the Japanese for spiritual reasons. In many villages in Japan, people are afraid of leaving their homes at night for fear of the demon that comes down from the mountain. The myth implies that the eyes of the demons were light in color. The Japanese feel that if a dog has a light eye color, the dog will bring misfortune to the family.

The ears are "V"-shaped and usually covered with fine, soft hair. The ears may be the same color as the dog's coat, slightly darker or black in color. Tosa ears are considered drop ears, which means they are not erect.

NECK
Muscular with a dewlap.

The neck is thick and muscular. The dewlap of the male Tosa is more prominent than that of the female. The area of the lower crest of the neck, withers and back contains some wrinkling, especially in males.

BODY
Withers: High.

Many of the Mastiff breeds are brachycephalic, and all have impressive, powerful heads. The Tosa is certainly no exception!

Back: Level and straight.

Loins: Broad, muscular.

Croup: Slightly arched at the top.

Chest: Broad and deep, ribs moderately sprung.

Belly: Well drawn up.

Even though the Tosa has loose skin, its belly is well drawn up, which gives it a more athletic appearance than the English Mastiff.

TAIL
Thick at the root, tapering towards the tip, reaching the hocks when let down.

LIMBS
Forequarters: Shoulder: Moderately sloping. Forearm: Straight, moderately long and strong. Pastern: Slightly inclining and robust.

The Tosa has strong bone structure and the legs are muscular.

Hindquarters: Muscles very developed, joints of stifle and hock moderately angulated, strong.

FEET
Tightly closed. Pads thick and elastic. Nails hard and preferably dark in color.

The feet are upright, tightly

knit and well knuckled (arched). The Japanese breeders most likely preferred the dark color of the nails because dark nails are harder and stronger than light-colored nails. Most breeds have larger front feet and carry the majority of their weight in their front ends.

GAIT

Robust and powerful.

The Tosa has a smooth, flowing and powerful gait. The breed has good drive from behind and is very athletic. The Tosa should have well-developed muscle in the rear end. This breed has great agility, especially for its size.

COAT

Hair: Short, hard and dense.

Hair coarseness can vary in the breed, from somewhat hard to very soft.

Color: Red, fawn, apricot, black, brindle. Slight white markings on chest and feet are permitted.

SIZE

Minimum height at withers for dogs 23.5 in (60 cm), for bitches 21.5 in (55 cm).

Tosas were classified as lightweight, middleweight and heavyweight for the fighting ring. Currently there is a great variation in the weight, overall size and bone density in this breed.

FAULTS

Any departure from the foregoing points should be considered as a fault and the seriousness with which the fault should be regarded should be in exact proportion to its degree.

- Thin bone.
- Snipy muzzle.
- Slightly overshot or under shot bite.

Excessive white markings are not desired in this breed.

The Tosa's back should be level and straight, and the belly is well drawn up.

Disqualifying Faults:

- Extremely overshot or undershot bite.
- Shyness.

NOTE

Male animals should have two apparently normal testicles fully descended into the scrotum.

JAPANESE TOSA

PUPPY SELECTION

Although the Tosa breeder has a large responsibility in making sure you get a puppy that is healthy and temperamentally sound, it is just as critical that you communicate with the breeder about your expectations, both for a puppy and for the life of your Tosa. Do you want a breeding dog, a show dog, a dog that is great with children, a dog to guard the house or business? Are you going to breed your Tosa or will you agree to spay or neuter? Is size, markings or color the most important aspect or are you more concerned with temperament? What do you mean (and what does the breeder

When selecting a Tosa puppy, there are usually lots to pick from. Tosa litters can be as large as 14 puppies!

TIME TO GO HOME
Breeders rarely release puppies until they are eight to ten weeks of age. This is an acceptable age for most breeds of dog, excepting toy breeds, which are not released until around 12 weeks, given their petite sizes. If a breeder has a puppy that is 12 weeks of age or older, it is likely well social-ized and house-trained. Be sure that it is otherwise healthy before deciding to take it home.

mean) by good temperament? Have you had experience with large dogs before or are you a novice with the giant breeds?

All of these considerations, if freely discussed with your breeder, can help to ensure that you get a Tosa that is best suited to your lifestyle, your family and your expectations. Part of the responsibility of the breeder is to ask you these questions; your responsibility is to have thought about the answers, discussed them with your family and clearly communicated them to your breeder. In every instance, however infrequent, that we have found an unfavorable match between the Tosa and his new home, it was a result of unclear or unexpressed expectations and wishes.

Although Tosa breeders are not as plentiful as breeders of more well-known breeds, it is still important to be choosy in selecting a breeder. You will most likely be in contact with the breeder throughout your Tosa's life, especially if you are co-owners or have a breeding or show Tosa. You should be comfortable with the breeder you choose, both professionally and personally.

Look for a breeder who asks you as many questions as you ask him. A breeder who is just interested in a sale will tell you whatever you want to hear. If he is genuinely interested in the dogs and the breed, he will ask you many questions. Don't be offended if he asks you questions that seem personal, because he is screening you as a prospective owner just as you are screening him. He will want to know about your lifestyle, home, family, work hours, previous dog experience and many other things. It is not unusual for breeders and prospective owners to spend several hours on the phone or in person getting to know each other.

Other things to consider: Does the breeder provide a

TEMPERAMENT COUNTS
Your selection of a good puppy can be determined by your needs. A show potential or a good pet? It is your choice. Every puppy, however, should be of good temperament. Although show-quality puppies are bred and raised with emphasis on physical conformation, responsible breeders strive for equally good temperament. Do not buy from a breeder who concentrates solely on physical beauty at the expense of personality.

health and temperament guarantee? What are the terms of the sale? Is he advertising only locally (possibly a sign of a novice breeder) or nationally, or even internationally? Will he allow you to tour his facility? This will give you a good idea of the care and attention given to his dogs.

LITTER SIZE

The average litter size is 6–8 pups, although we have had litters as large as 14 and as small as 2. Our experience is that in very large litters, the pups need more attention to be sure that they all get opportunities to nurse. The weaker pups may not be able to get enough milk on their own to grow properly. In addition, a large litter is very hard on the dam and she is sometimes not able to provide enough nourishment to the pups. In a very small litter, the biggest problem is that the puppies may get too much nourishment and tend to be too heavy for their own good health. In any litter, the breeder must watch the nursing habits of the puppies carefully.

By the time you are ready to pick out your Tosa pup, at about seven to eight weeks of age, your breeder will be a great guide in helping you select the pup that most closely matches your needs. The breeder will be very familiar with each pup's physical attributes and temperament. For potential show or breeding dogs, your breeder can point out physical traits that would make a superior candidate: bone structure, a good head, movement, etc. This can assist you in choosing just the right puppy.

But don't buy a Tosa on looks alone. You and your breeder should consider the temperament of the individual puppies. Tosas are by nature loyal, trustworthy and confident. But there are differences in individuals. Some tend to be more dominant, some are more attentive and responsive to affection. None should be shy or spooky, even at this early age. Since you will have discussed your needs with the breeder, he should be very willing and able to guide you in selecting the best Tosa pup for you and your family.

However, good breeding and sound temperament will all be lost if you, as the new owner, don't provide training, guidance and a good foundation for your pup. A puppy, just like a child, cannot make his way in the world without adult guidance.

In deciding upon a male or a female, there are some physical considerations, the most obvious of which is size. The male Tosa is, on average, about 30 lb (14 kg) heavier than the females. Males have blockier heads and larger bone than females. They

We have found that in a Tosa litter, the dominant puppy could be either a male or a female. This greatly depends on the individual temperament of the puppies. One characteristic of a male Tosa is that, while he normally will not "pick a fight" with a smaller dog, he also will not back down if another dog challenges him. Therefore, it is easier to take females out in public to places where there is a chance of meeting other dogs.

COMMITMENT OF OWNERSHIP
After considering all of the factors that have led to your choice of the Tosa, you also have most likely already made some very important decisions about selecting your puppy. You have decided that the Tosa is the breed for you, which means that

also tend to have more wrinkles and because of this will drool more. Both males and females are giant dogs.

Temperamentally, both sexes are wonderful with families and with children, showing great patience and tolerance for the unexpected and erratic activities of families. Both sexes are very protective of their home territories. What we have found interesting is that when a male and a female Tosa live together, it is usually the female who takes the lead in guarding and alerting us to strangers. This may be due to the females' natural instinct for guarding that comes from the mothering instinct.

A wheelbarrow of Japanese delight! The acquisition of a Tosa is one-part fun and nine-parts responsibility.

PEDIGREE VS. REGISTRATION CERTIFICATE

Too often new owners are confused between these two important documents. Your puppy's pedigree, essentially a family tree, is a written record of a dog's genealogy of three generations or more. The pedigree will show you the names as well as performance titles of all the dogs in your pup's background. Your breeder must provide you with a registration application, with his part properly filled out. You must complete the application and send it to the registering organization with the proper fee. Every puppy must come from a litter that has been registered by the breeder and from a sire and dam that are also registered.

The seller must provide you with complete records to identify the puppy. The registry requires that the seller provide the buyer with the following: breed; sex, color and markings; date of birth; litter number (when available); names and registration numbers of the parents; breeder's name; and date sold or delivered.

Narrowing down your selection requires you to discuss your wants and desires with the breeder as honestly as possible. The breeder will steer you to the puppy that will best fit into your living situation and family.

you have decided which characteristics you want in a dog and what type of dog will best fit into your family and lifestyle. If you have selected a breeder, you have gone a step further—you have done your research and found a responsible, conscientious person who breeds quality Tosas and who should be a reli-

able source of help as you and your puppy adjust to life together. If you have observed a litter in action, you have obtained a firsthand look at the dynamics of a puppy "pack" and, thus, you have learned about each pup's individual personality—perhaps you have even found one that particularly appeals to you.

However, even if you have not yet found the Tosa puppy of your dreams, observing pups will help you learn to recognize certain behaviors and to determine what a pup's behavior indicates about his temperament. You will be able to pick out which pups are the leaders, which ones are less outgoing, which ones are confident, which ones are shy, playful, friendly, aggressive, etc. Equally as important, you will learn to recognize

what a healthy pup should look and act like. All of these things will help you in your search, and when you find the Tosa that was meant for you, you will know it!

Researching your breed, selecting a responsible breeder and observing as many pups as possible are all important steps on the way to dog ownership. It may seem like a lot of effort... and you have not even taken the pup home yet! Remember,

ARE YOU PREPARED?

Unfortunately, when a puppy is bought by someone who does not take into consideration the time and attention that dog ownership requires, it is the puppy who suffers when he is either abandoned or placed in a shelter by a frustrated owner. So all of the "homework" you do in preparation for your pup's arrival will benefit you both. The more informed you are, the more you will know what to expect and the better equipped you will be to handle the ups and downs of raising a puppy. Hopefully, everyone in the household is willing to do his part in raising and caring for the pup. The anticipation of owning a dog often brings a lot of promises from excited family members: "I will walk him every day," "I will feed him," "I will house-train him," etc., but these things take time and effort, and promises can easily be forgotten once the novelty of the new pet has worn off.

though, you cannot be too careful when it comes to deciding on the type of dog you want and finding out about your prospective pup's background. Buying a puppy is not—or *should* not be—just another whimsical purchase. This is one instance in which you actually do get to choose your own family! You may be thinking that buying a puppy should be fun—it should not be so serious and so much work. Keep in mind that your puppy is not a cuddly stuffed toy or decorative lawn ornament; rather, he is a living creature who will become a real member of your family. You will come to realize that, while buying a puppy is a pleasurable and exciting endeavor, it is not something to be taken lightly. Relax...the fun will start when the pup comes home!

Always keep in mind that a puppy is nothing more than a

Watching a pup with one of his parents tells much about the temperament of the bloodline, and also helps you to predict the pup's adult looks and size.

baby in a furry disguise…a baby who is virtually helpless in a human world and who trusts his owner for fulfillment of his basic needs for survival. In addition to food, water and shelter, your pup needs care, protection, guidance and love. If you are not prepared to commit to this, then you are not prepared to own a dog.

"Wait a minute," you say.

HANDLE WITH CARE
You should be extremely careful about handling tiny puppies. Not that you might hurt them, but that the pups' mother may exhibit what is called "maternal aggression." It is a natural, instinctive reaction for the dam to protect her young against anything she interprets as predatory or possibly harmful to pups. The sweetest, most gentle of bitches, after whelping a litter, often reacts this way, even to her owner.

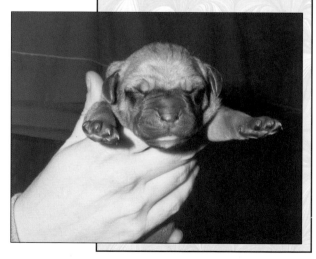

"How hard could this be? All of my neighbors own dogs and they seem to be doing just fine. Why should I have to worry about all of this?" Well, you should not worry about it; in fact, you will probably find that once your Tosa pup gets used to his new home, he will fall into his place in the family quite naturally. However, it never hurts to emphasize the commitment of dog ownership. With some time and patience, it is really not too difficult to raise a curious and exuberant Tosa pup to be a well-adjusted and well-mannered adult dog—a dog that could be your most loyal friend.

PREPARING PUPPY'S PLACE IN YOUR HOME
Researching your breed and finding a breeder are only two aspects of the "homework" you will have to do before taking your Tosa puppy home. You will also have to prepare your home and family for the new addition. Much as you would prepare a nursery for a newborn baby, you will need to designate a place in your home that will be the puppy's own. How you prepare your home will depend on how much freedom the dog will be allowed. Whatever you decide, you must ensure that he has a place that he can "call his own."

When you bring your new puppy into your home, you are

PET INSURANCE

Just like you can insure your car, your house and your own health, you likewise can insure your dog's health. Investigate a pet insurance policy by talking to your vet. Depending on the age of your dog, the breed and the kind of coverage you desire, your policy can be very affordable. Most policies cover accidental injuries, poisoning and thousands of medical problems and illnesses, including cancers. Some carriers also offer routine care and immunization coverage.

it, but the sudden shock of being transplanted is somewhat traumatic for a young pup. Imagine how a small child would feel in the same situation—this is how your puppy must be feeling. It is up to you to reassure him and to let him know, "Little *inu*, you are going to like it here!"

WHAT YOU SHOULD BUY

CRATE

To someone unfamiliar with the use of crates in dog training, it may seem like punishment to

bringing him into what will become his home as well. Obviously, you did not buy a puppy with the intentions of catering to his every whim and allowing him to "rule the roost," but in order for a puppy to grow into a stable, well-adjusted dog, he has to feel comfortable in his surroundings. Remember, he is leaving the warmth and security of his mother and littermates, as well as the familiarity of the only place he has ever known, so it is important to make his transition as easy as possible. By preparing a place in your home for the puppy, you are making him feel as welcome as possible in a strange new place. It should not take him long to get used to

Are your home and family ready for this giant addition? Keep in mind that your small puppy will grow into a massive guard dog before your eyes!

Your local pet shop will have a variety of crates. Get the largest one available for your Tosa.

PHOTO COURTESY OF DOSKOCIL.

training is a very popular and very successful house-training method. In addition, a crate can keep your dog safe during travel and, perhaps most importantly, a crate provides your dog with a place of his own in your home. It serves as a "doggie bedroom" of sorts—your Tosa can curl up in his crate when he wants to sleep or when he just needs a break. Many dogs sleep in their crates overnight. With soft bedding and his favorite toy, a crate becomes a cozy pseudo-den for your dog. Like his ancestors, he too will seek out the comfort and retreat

CRATE-TRAINING TIPS

During crate training, you should partition off the section of the crate in which the pup stays. If he is given too big an area, this will hinder your training efforts. Crate training is based on the fact that a dog does not like to soil his sleeping quarters, so it is ineffective to keep a pup in an area that is so big that he can eliminate in one end and get far enough away from it to sleep. Also, you want to make the crate den-like for the pup. Blankets and a favorite toy will make the crate cozy for the small pup; as he grows, you may want to evict some of his "roommates" to make more room. It will take some coaxing at first, but be patient. Given some time to get used to it, your pup will adapt to his new home-within-a-home quite nicely.

shut a dog in a crate, but this is not the case at all. Although all breeders do not advocate crate training, more and more breeders and trainers are recommending crates as preferred tools for pet puppies as well as show puppies.

Crates are not cruel—crates have many humane and highly effective uses in dog care and training. For example, crate

of a den—you just happen to be providing him with something a little more luxurious than what his early ancestors enjoyed.

As far as purchasing a crate, the type that you buy is up to you. It will most likely be one of the two most popular types: wire or fiberglass. There are advantages and disadvantages to each type. For example, a wire crate is more open, allowing the air to flow through and affording the dog a view of what is going on around him, while a fiberglass crate is sturdier. Both can double as travel crates, providing protection for the dog during transport.

The size of the crate is another thing to consider. We use the largest crates possible, a 700 crate for a mature adult male. Smaller females (up to 120 lb) may do well in a 500 crate, especially if the crate is just to be used as a sleeping den. A good rule of thumb is that the dog should be able to stand up and turn around comfortably in the crate.

BEDDING

A crate pad in the dog's crate will help the dog feel more at home, and you may also like to give him a small blanket. First, these will take the place of the leaves, twigs, etc., that the pup would use in the wild to make a den; the pup can make his own "burrow" in the crate. Although your pup is far removed from his den-making ancestors, the denning instinct is still a part of his genetic makeup. Second, until you take your pup home, he has been sleeping amid the warmth of his mother and littermates, and while a blanket is not the same as a warm, breathing body, it still provides heat and something with which to snuggle. You will want to wash your pup's bedding frequently in case

When looking at a tiny baby Tosa, it's amazing to imagine the strong and massive dog he will grow up to be.

TOYS, TOYS, TOYS!

With a big variety of dog toys available, and so many that look like they would be a lot of fun for a dog, be careful in your selection. It is amazing what a set of puppy teeth can do to an innocent-looking toy; so, obviously, safety is a major consideration. Be sure to choose the most durable products that you can find. Hard nylon bones and toys are a safe bet, and many of them are offered in different scents and flavors that will be sure to capture your dog's attention. It is always fun to play a game of fetch with your dog, and there are balls and flying discs that are specially made to withstand dog teeth.

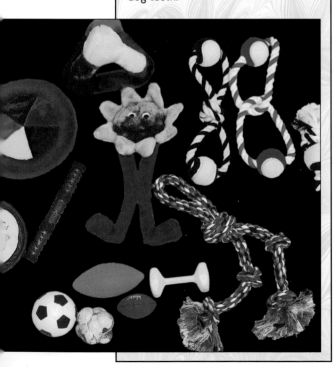

he has a potty "accident" in his crate, and replace or remove any blanket or padding that becomes ragged and starts to fall apart.

CHEW TOYS

Since chewing is a part of every dog's development, appropriate safe chew toys are a must. Some Tosas may chew more than others, but this is not characteristic of the breed. We have found this trait to be extremely variable. Some dogs start chewing later in life, and some puppies develop the habit and soon outgrow it. Sometimes older dogs may find joy in seeking out hoses or shoes to gnaw on. Some Tosas delight in "sculpting" the edges of their doghouses by chewing them into unique patterns. The amazing thing is that many of the products that are designed to prevent dogs from chewing (such as bitter sprays) won't slow a Tosa down at all. You can try to experiment to find one that works. If a Tosa develops a chewing habit, it is not from instinct or genetics; it is usually a bad habit that requires creative attention on the owner's part in order to eliminate. Chewing may also point to a nutritional deficiency.

For an inexpensive and readily available toy for puppies, empty plastic bottles (remove and discard the screw caps) can amuse a Tosa pup for hours; they

FINANCIAL RESPONSIBILITY

Grooming tools, collars, leashes, a crate, a dog bed and, of course, toys will be expenses to you when you first obtain your pup, and the cost will continue throughout your dog's lifetime. If your puppy damages or destroys your possessions (as most puppies surely will!) or something belonging to a neighbor, you can calculate additional expense. There is also flea and pest control, which every dog owner faces more than once. You must be able to handle the financial responsibility of owning a dog.

are chewy, make noise and seem to have lives of their own. Many times, when investigating why a puppy is barking so animatedly, we will find him playing rambunctiously with a plastic bottle. Of course, a puppy can easily destroy a plastic bottle, so the bottle should be removed from the puppy before it is torn into pieces.

A sturdy ball attached to a rope tug is safe and fun. The knotted rope toys are favorites with Tosas. Try the rubber toys that can hold kibble or peanut butter for a real treat—Tosas love to figure out how to get the goodies out. Tosas may like to run after balls or frisbees, but don't expect to get these objects back—retrievers they are not. Stay away from small balls (like tennis balls)

that can easily be ripped apart and swallowed. Some books advise against playing tug-of-war with large dogs because of their strength, but we have found that this is a great game to play for both human and dog. It requires skill, strength and awareness. Just remember to carefully monitor the condition of all of your Tosa's toys, and remove and replace any that are worn to the point of becoming dangerous.

LEASH

A nylon leash is probably the best option, as it is the most resistant to puppy teeth should your pup take a liking to chewing on his leash. Of course, this is a habit that should be nipped in the bud, but, if your pup likes to chew on his leash, he has a very slim chance of being able to

Pet shops usually stock a wide assortment of leashes from which you can select a sturdy leash for your Tosa.

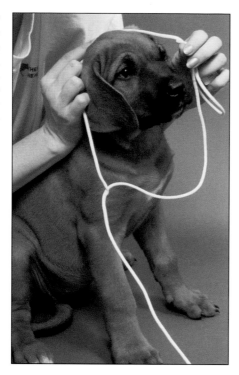

The show puppy can be trained to work with a thin nylon lead, though this device is not suitable for everyday walks or training sessions.

chew through the strong nylon. Nylon leashes are also strong but lightweight, which is good for a young Tosa who is just getting used to the idea of walking on a leash. For everyday walking and safety purposes, the nylon leash is a good choice.

As your Tosa grows up and grows stronger, you will need to purchase a larger, stronger leash, such as very thick nylon or thick leather. Flexible leashes are popular with owners of many breeds, but do not provide the control necessary for large breeds and are not suitable for use with the Tosa.

COLLAR

Your pup should get used to wearing a collar all of the time since you will want to attach his ID tags to it; plus, you have to attach the leash to something! A lightweight adjustable nylon collar is a good choice. Make certain that the collar fits snugly enough so that the pup cannot wriggle out of it, but is loose enough so that it will not be uncomfortably tight around the pup's neck. You should be able to fit a finger between the pup's neck and the collar. It may take some time for your pup to get used to wearing the collar, but soon he will not even notice that it is there. Choke collars are made for training and are recommended for the Tosa. Be sure you learn how to properly use the choke collar before putting it on your dog.

FOOD AND WATER BOWLS

Your pup will need two bowls, one for food and one for water. You may want two sets of bowls, one for indoors and one for outdoors, depending on where the dog will be fed and where he will be spending time. Stainless steel or sturdy plastic bowls are popular choices. Plastic bowls are more chewable, but dogs tend not to chew on the steel variety, which can be sterilized. It is important to buy sturdy bowls since anything is in

Pet shops carry a wide selection of bowls for food and water. Buy the largest sizes available for your Tosa, along with stands on which to elevate them.

danger of being chewed by puppy teeth and you do not want your dog to be constantly chewing apart his bowl (for his safety and for your wallet!).

It is also recommended to purchase or make stands on which to elevate your Tosa's bowl. This is a good bloat preventative, as the dog does not have to crane his neck to reach his bowls and, thus, will not swallow as much air while eating and drinking.

CLEANING SUPPLIES
Until a pup is house-trained, you will be doing a lot of cleaning. "Accidents" will occur, which is acceptable in the beginning stages of potty training because the puppy does not know any better. All you can do is be prepared to clean up any accidents as soon as they happen. Old rags, paper towels, newspapers and a safe disinfectant are good to have on hand.

BEYOND THE BASICS

The items previously discussed are the bare necessities. You will find out what else you need as you go along—grooming supplies, flea/tick protection, baby gates to partition a room, etc. These things will vary depending on your situation, but it is important that you have everything you need to feed and make your Tosa comfortable in his first few days at home.

This impressive head belongs to the giant male Bidanshi of Temahimeden, who weighs in at an impressive 198.5 lb (90 kg) and stands just over 36 in (92 cm).

PUPPY-PROOFING YOUR HOME

Aside from making sure that your Tosa will be comfortable in your home, you also have to make sure that your home is safe for your Tosa. This means taking precautions that your pup will not get into anything he should not get into and that there is nothing within his reach that may harm him should he sniff it, chew it, inspect it, etc. This probably seems obvious since, while you are primarily concerned with your pup's safety, at the same time you do not want your belongings to be ruined. Breakables should be placed out of reach if your dog is to have full run of the house. If he is to be limited to certain places within the house, keep any potentially dangerous items in the "off-limits" areas.

An electrical cord can pose a danger should the puppy decide to taste it—and who is going to convince a pup that it would not make a great chew toy? Cords should be fastened tightly against the wall, away from the pup. If your dog is going to spend time in a crate, make sure that there is nothing near his crate that he can reach if he sticks his curious little paws through the openings. Just as you would with a child, keep all household cleaners and chemicals where the pup cannot reach them.

It is also important to make sure that the outside of your home is safe. Of course, your puppy should never be unsupervised, but a pup let loose in the yard will want to run and explore, and he should be granted that freedom. Tosas are not by nature climbers, jumpers or diggers. They usually respect boundaries and will not climb or jump over a fence even if it would be easy for them to do so. A 6-foot fence should be more than adequate.

Keep the dog's house away from the fence; we have had Tosas who, while exploring, stood on the top of the doghouse, looked over the fence and then just found themselves in the neighbor's yard. However, Tosas don't dig to dig their way out; rather, they will dig to find a cool place to lie or to bury their treasured items.

FIRST TRIP TO THE VET

You have selected your puppy, and your home and family are ready. Now all you have to do is collect your Tosa from the breeder and the fun begins, right? Well...not so fast. Something else you need to plan is your pup's first trip to the veterinarian. Perhaps the breeder can recommend someone in the area who specializes in giant breeds, or maybe you know some other dog owners who can

NATURAL TOXINS
Examine your grass and landscaping before bringing your puppy home. Many varieties of plants have leaves, stems or flowers that are toxic if ingested, and you can depend on a curious puppy to investigate them. Ask your vet for information on poisonous plants or research them at your library.

suggest a good vet. Either way, you should have an appointment arranged for your pup before you pick him up.

The pup's first visit will consist of an overall examination to make sure that the pup does

Your new Tosa puppy will require encouragement and love upon coming to your home. All puppies feel "out of place" when first transplanted to their human families.

not have any problems that are not apparent to you. The vet will also set up a schedule for the pup's vaccinations; the breeder will inform you of which ones the pup has already received and the vet can continue from there.

INTRODUCTION TO THE FAMILY

Everyone in the house will be excited about the puppy's coming home and will want to pet him and play with him, but it is best to make the introductions low-key so as not to overwhelm the puppy. He is apprehensive already. It is the first

time he has been separated from his dam and the breeder, and the ride to your home is likely to be the first time he has been in a car. The last thing you want to do is smother him, as this will only frighten him further. This is not to say that human contact is not extremely necessary at this stage, because this is the time when a connection between the pup and his human family is formed. Gentle petting and soothing words should help console him, as well as just putting him down and letting him explore on his own (under your watchful eye, of course).

The pup may approach the family members or may busy himself with exploring for a while. Gradually, each person should spend some time with the pup, one at a time, crouching down to get as close to the pup's level as possible, letting him sniff their hands and petting him gently. He definitely needs human attention and he needs to

CHEMICAL TOXINS
Scour your garage for potential puppy dangers. Remove weed killers, pesticides and antifreeze materials. Antifreeze is highly toxic and just a few drops can kill a puppy or an adult dog. The sweet taste attracts the animal, who will quickly consume it from the floor or pavement.

be touched—this is how to form an immediate bond. Just remember that the pup is experiencing many things for the first time, at the same time. There are new people, new noises, new smells and new things to investigate, so be gentle, be affectionate and be as comforting as you can be.

PUP'S FIRST NIGHT HOME

You have traveled home with your new charge safely in his crate. He's been to the vet for a thorough check-up; he's been weighed, his papers have been examined and perhaps he's even been vaccinated and wormed as well. He's met (and licked!) the whole family, including the excited children and the less-than-happy cat. He's explored his area, his new bed, the yard and anywhere else he's been permitted. He's eaten his first meal at home and relieved himself in the proper place. He's heard lots of new sounds, smelled new friends and seen more of the outside world than ever before…and that was just the first day! He's worn out and is ready for bed…or so you think!

It's puppy's first night home and you are ready to say "Good night." Keep in mind that this is his first night ever to be sleeping alone. His dam and littermates are no longer at paw's length and he's a bit scared, cold and lonely.

HOW VACCINES WORK

If you've just bought a puppy, you surely know the importance of having your pup vaccinated, but do you understand how vaccines work? Vaccines contain the same bacteria or viruses that cause the disease you want to prevent, but they have been chemically modified so that they don't cause any harm. Instead, the vaccine causes your dog to produce antibodies that fight the harmful bacteria. Thus, if your dog is exposed to the disease in the future, the antibodies will destroy the viruses or bacteria.

Be reassuring to your new family member, but this is not the time to spoil him and give in to his inevitable whining.

Puppies whine. They whine to let others know where they are and hopefully to get company out of it. Place your pup in his new bed or crate in his designated area and close the door. Mercifully, he may fall asleep without a peep. When the inevitable occurs, however, ignore the whining—he is fine. Be strong and keep his best interest in mind. Do not allow yourself to feel guilty and visit the pup. He will fall asleep eventually.

Many breeders recommend placing a piece of bedding from the pup's former home in his new bed so that he recognizes and is comforted by the scent of his littermates. Others still advise placing a hot water bottle in the bed for warmth. The latter may be a good idea, provided the pup doesn't attempt to suckle—he'll get good and wet, and may not fall asleep so fast.

Puppy's first night can be somewhat stressful for both the pup and his new family. Remember that you are setting

"Little Tosa, you're going to like it here!" Make your Tosa feel comfortable in his new home, but don't surrender the whole empire to him right away!

STRESS-FREE
Some experts in canine health advise that stress during a dog's early years of development can compromise and weaken his immune system, and may trigger the potential for a shortened life. They emphasize the need for happy and stress-free growing-up years.

the tone of nighttime at your house. Unless you want to play with your pup every night at 10 p.m., midnight and 2 a.m., don't initiate the habit. Your family will thank you, and eventually so will your pup!

PREVENTING PUPPY PROBLEMS

SOCIALIZATION

Now that you have done all of the preparatory work and have helped your pup get accustomed to his new home and family, it is about time for you to have some fun! Socializing your Tosa pup gives you the opportunity to show off your new friend, and your pup gets to reap the benefits of being an adorable creature that people will want to pet and, in general, think is absolutely precious!

Besides getting to know his new family, your puppy should be exposed to other people, animals and situations. This will help him become well adjusted as he grows up and less prone to being timid or fearful of the new things he will encounter. Of course, he must not come into close contact with dogs you don't know well until his course of injections is fully complete.

Your pup's socialization began with the breeder, but now it is your responsibility to continue it. The socialization he receives until the age of 12 weeks is the most critical, as this is the time when he forms his impressions of the outside world. Be especially careful during the eight-to-ten-week-old period, also known as the fear period. The interaction he receives during this time should be gentle and reassuring. Lack of socialization, and/or negative experiences during the socialization period, can manifest itself in fear and aggression as the dog grows up. Your puppy needs lots of positive interaction, which of course includes human contact, affection, handling and exposure to other animals.

Once your pup has received his necessary vaccinations, feel free to take him out and about (on his leash, of course). Walk him around the neighborhood, take him on your daily errands, let people pet him, let him meet other dogs and pets, etc. Puppies do not have to try to make

IN DUE TIME
It will take at least two weeks for your puppy to become accustomed to his new surroundings. Give him lots of love, attention, handling, frequent opportunities to relieve himself, a diet he likes to eat and a place he can call his own.

friends; there will be no shortage of people who will want to introduce themselves. Just make sure that you carefully supervise each meeting. If the neighborhood children want to say hello, for example, that is great—children and pups most often make great companions. However, sometimes an excited child can unintentionally handle a pup too roughly, or an overzealous pup can playfully nip a little too hard.

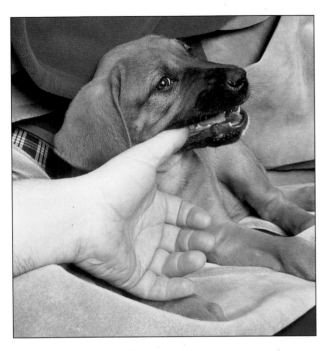

"pack" is entirely up to you! Your pup's intuitive quest for dominance, coupled with the fact that it is nearly impossible to look at an adorable Tosa pup with his "puppy-dog" eyes and not cave in, give the pup almost an unfair advantage in getting the upper hand! A pup will definitely test the waters to see what he can and cannot do. Do not give in to those pleading eyes—stand your ground when it comes to disciplining the pup and make sure that all family members do the same. It will only confuse the pup if Mother tells him to get off the sofa when he is used to sitting up there with Father to watch the nightly news. Avoid

Part of owning a puppy means dealing with puppy teeth! Nipping is a common puppy behavior, but one that should be discouraged firmly and consistently.

You want to make socialization experiences positive ones. What a pup learns during this very formative stage will affect his attitude toward future encounters. You want your dog to be comfortable around everyone. A pup that has a bad experience with a child may grow up to be a dog that is shy around or aggressive toward children.

CONSISTENCY IN TRAINING

Dogs, being pack animals, naturally need a leader, or else they try to establish dominance in their packs. When you welcome a dog into your family, the choice of who becomes the leader and who becomes the

PLAY'S THE THING

Teaching the puppy to play with his toys in running and fetching games is an ideal way to help the puppy develop muscle, learn motor skills and bond with you, his owner and master. He also needs to learn how to inhibit his bite reflex and never to use his teeth on people, forbidden objects and other animals in play. Whenever you play with your puppy, you make the rules. This becomes an important message to your puppy in teaching him that you are the pack leader and control everything he does in life. Once your dog accepts you as his leader, your relationship with him will be cemented for life.

discrepancies by having all members of the household decide on the rules before the pup even comes home...and be consistent in enforcing them! Early training shapes the dog's personality, so you cannot be unclear in what you expect.

COMMON PUPPY PROBLEMS

The best way to prevent puppy problems is to be proactive in stopping an undesirable behavior as soon as it starts. The old saying "You can't teach an old dog new tricks" does not necessarily hold true, but it *is* true that it is much easier to discourage bad behavior in a young developing pup than to wait until the pup's bad behavior

THE COCOA WARS
Chocolate contains the chemical thebromine, which is poisonous to dogs, although "chocolates" especially made for dogs are safe (as they don't actually contain chocolate) but not recommended. Any item that encourages your dog to enjoy the taste of cocoa should be discouraged. You should also exercise caution when using mulch in your garden. This frequently contains cocoa hulls, and dogs have been known to die from eating the mulch.

becomes the adult dog's bad habit. There are some problems that are especially prevalent in puppies as they develop.

These two youngsters couldn't be more pleased to have a loyal protector like the Tosa, and they don't even mind being dwarfed by their massive canine companion.

BEWARE

CHEWING TIPS

Chewing goes hand in hand with nipping in the sense that a teething puppy is always looking for a way to soothe his aching gums. In this case, instead of chewing on you, he may have taken a liking to your favorite shoe or something else that he should not be chewing. Again, realize that this is a normal canine behavior that does not need to be discouraged, only redirected. Your pup just needs to be taught what is acceptable to chew on and what is off-limits. Consistently tell him "No!" when you catch him chewing on something forbidden and give him a chew toy.

Conversely, praise him when you catch him chewing on something appropriate. In this way, you are discouraging the inappropriate behavior and reinforcing the desired behavior. The puppy's chewing should stop after his adult teeth have come in, but an adult dog continues to chew for various reasons—perhaps because he is bored, needs to relieve tension or just likes to chew. That is why it is important to redirect his chewing when he is still young.

NIPPING

As puppies start to teethe, they feel the need to sink their teeth into anything available...unfortunately, that usually includes your fingers, arms, hair and toes. You may find this behavior cute for the first five seconds...until you feel just how sharp those puppy teeth are. Nipping is something you want to discourage immediately and consistently with a firm "No!" (or whatever number of firm "Nos" it takes for him to understand that you mean business). Then, replace your finger with an appropriate chew toy. While this behavior is merely annoying when the dog is young, it can become dangerous as your Tosa's adult teeth grow in and his jaws develop, and he continues to think it is okay to gnaw on human appendages. Your Tosa does not mean any harm with a friendly nip, but he also does not know the strength of his large teeth and jaws.

CRYING/WHINING

Your pup will often cry, whine, whimper, howl or make some type of commotion when he is left alone. This is basically his way of calling out for attention to make sure that you know he is there and that you have not forgotten about him. Your puppy feels insecure when he is left alone, when you are out of the house and he is in his crate or when you are in another part of the house and he cannot see you. The noise he is making is an expression of the anxiety he feels at being alone, so he needs to be taught that being alone is okay.

Even a giant dog like the Tosa starts out as a small puppy who has to find his place in a big world. Supervise all of your puppy's explorations, indoors and out.

You are not actually training the dog to stop making noise; rather, you are training him to feel comfortable when he is alone and thus removing the need for him to make the noise.

This is where the crate with cozy bedding and a toy comes in handy. You want to know that your pup is safe when you are not there to supervise, and you know that he will be safe in his crate rather than roaming freely about the house. In order for the pup to stay in his crate without making a fuss, he first needs to be comfortable in his crate. On that note, it is extremely important that the crate is never used as a form of punishment; this will cause the pup to view the crate as a negative place rather than as a place of his own for safety and retreat.

Accustom the pup to the crate in short, gradually increasing time intervals in which you put him in the crate, maybe with a treat, and stay in the room with him. If he cries or makes a fuss, do not go to him, but stay in his sight. Gradually he will realize that staying in his crate is just fine without your help, and it will not be so traumatic for him when you are not around. You may want to leave the radio on softly when you leave the house; the sound of human voices may be comforting to him.

DIETARY AND FEEDING CONSIDERATIONS

As people become more aware of how their own diets affect their health and well-being, they are realizing that the same holds true for their dogs. Dogs can't choose what or when they eat, and so an owner has a special responsibility to his dog to provide him with the best possible diet. But what makes up a healthy diet?

When a conscientious dog owner tries to get information about the best food or supplements for his dog, he finds that there are as many opinions as there are breeds of dog, each one supported

---

STORING DOG FOOD
You must store your dry dog food carefully. Open packages of dog food quickly lose their vitamin value, usually within 90 days of being opened. Mold spores and vermin could also contaminate the food.

---

by some sort of research. With the growth of the pet industry in recent years, there has been a proliferation of magazines and journals dedicated to dogs and their owners. It is rare to find any publication that doesn't contain information about how to feed and supplement your dog for optimal

Chow time for a hungry Tosa litter!

FOOD PREFERENCE

Selecting the best dry dog food is difficult. There is no majority consensus among veterinary scientists as to the value of nutrient analysis (protein, fat, fiber, moisture, ash, cholesterol, minerals, etc.). All agree that feeding trials are what matter most, but you also have to consider the individual dog. The dog's weight, age and activity level, and what pleases his taste, all must be considered. It is best to take the advice of your veterinarian and breeder. Every dog's dietary requirements vary, even during the lifetime of a particular dog.

If your dog is fed a good complete dry food, it does not require supplements of meat or vegetables. Dogs do appreciate a little variety in their diets, so you may choose to stay with the same brand but vary the flavor. Alternatively, you may wish to add a little flavored stock to give a difference to the taste.

health. The problem for the average dog owner is that the experts often disagree, so how does an owner sort through the information?

There are three things to consider when deciding on a diet for your dog:
1) Health and physical requirements of the breed and of your individual dog;
2) Cost factors: Optimal food and supplements are expensive— you may not be able to afford the "best" of everything;
3) How much time do you have to devote to your dog's feeding?

Most commercial dog foods are prepared in three basic types: dry, semi-moist and canned. Raw-food diets, either home-made or commercially bought, have become more common and popular in recent years. Each diet has advantages and disadvantages as outlined in the following section. Our recommendation for large breeds like the Tosa is a diet of baked dry food, preserved using natural ingredients.

Dry Foods

Dry foods are the least expensive and most convenient, and for the Tosa owner may well be the best option. They have very long shelf lives due to low moisture content and use of preservatives. Traditional chemical preservatives (BHA and BHT) have been implicated in health problems in dogs, so, in

A little competition around the feeding bowl entices the puppies' appetites. Once your Tosa puppy is home alone, he may need a little encouragement at mealtime.

recent years, many brands have started using natural preservatives. But even with preservatives, dry food will lose many nutrients over time. If you choose dry food for your Tosa, buy and open only what you can use in two to three weeks. Keep it from getting too hot or too damp. Heat will cause even faster depletion of nutrients and rancidity; dampness will encourage growth of molds and bacteria. When feeding dry food to your Tosa, first moisten it slightly with lukewarm water.

Bonding with your Tosa puppy is akin to making your puppy understand that you are his leader, the one he must protect with his whole heart.

"DOES THIS COLLAR MAKE ME LOOK FAT?"

While humans may obsess about how they look and how trim their bodies are, many people believe that extra weight on their dogs is a good thing. The truth is, pets should not be over- or under-weight, as both can lead to or signal sickness. In order to tell how fit your pet is, run your hands over his ribs. Are his ribs buried under a layer of fat or are they sticking out considerably? If your pet is within his normal weight range, you should be able to feel the ribs easily, but they should not protrude abnormally. If you stand above him, the outline of his body should resemble an hourglass. Some breeds do tend to be leaner while some are a bit stockier, but making sure your dog is the right weight for his breed will certainly contribute to his good health.

A recent variation of dry foods are the "baked" types. These are cooked at lower temperatures than traditional dry foods and the manufacturers feel that more of the nutrient value of the food is preserved in this process. Baked foods are slightly more expensive per cup but, since they are denser and have higher nutrient content, dogs consume fewer cups per meal. Baked food is a good option when choosing a dry food.

The variety of dry foods is amazing. A complete discussion

would take pages, but here are a few tried-and-true suggestions. Avoid preservatives like BHA and BHT and use naturally preserved foods. Beet pulp, an indigestible fiber that absorbs water, is often used to create firmer stools in dogs. Many breeders and veterinarians who work with large and giant breeds do not recommend feeding this ingredient to dogs. It absorbs water even while in the dog's stomach and has been linked to cases of bloat (torsion). Breeders of large and giant breeds experienced a noticeable decrease

FEEDING TIPS

• Dog food must be served at room temperature, neither too hot nor too cold. Fresh water, changed often and served in a clean bowl, is mandatory, but limit water intake at mealtimes.
• Never feed your dog from the table while you are eating, and never feed your dog leftovers from your own meal. They usually contain too much fat and too much seasoning.
• Dogs must chew their food. Hard pellets are excellent; soups and stews are to be avoided.
• Don't add leftovers or any extras to commercial dog food. The normal food is usually balanced, and adding something extra destroys the balance.
• Except for age-related changes, dogs do not require dietary variations. They can be fed the same diet, day after day, without becoming bored or ill.

in incidences of bloat when foods with beet pulp as an ingredient were eliminated.

Avoid foods that have grains, like wheat, corn or rice, as the primary ingredient. Dogs are carnivores; grains should be a minimal portion of their diet. Read the entire label. Sometimes grain products are split up so that they appear to be less predominant; for example, wheat, wheat gluten, wheat bran and wheat flour may be listed as separate ingredients.

Good-quality protein like turkey, chicken, lamb or beef should be the first ingredient listed. Chicken, beef or lamb "meals" are generally favorable, high-quality sources of protein; meat or poultry "meals" are lower quality proteins and should be avoided when feeding your Tosa.

Limiting water intake around mealtimes and never allowing your Tosa to gulp water are important preventative measures against bloat.

Pregnant and lactating bitches may require dietary changes and special supplementation, any of which should only be done under a vet's guidance.

Foods with the terms "meat, animal or other by-products" may contain any parts of the animal, including indigestible proteins like feathers, guts and other organs, and are not recommended for your Tosa.

DO DOGS HAVE TASTE BUDS?

Watching a dog "wolf" or gobble his food, seemingly without chewing, leads an owner to wonder whether his dog can taste anything. Yes, dogs have taste buds, with sensory perception of sweet, salty and sour.

Puppies are born with fully mature taste buds.

CANNED AND SEMI-MOIST FOODS
Canned dog foods are 60 to 70% water, but the protein is usually higher quality than that in dry foods. Still, getting enough protein from canned food for your Tosa would most likely be too expensive. Our experience, corroborated by our vets, is that dogs that eat moist food have a greater build-up of plaque on their teeth and may require more frequent cleanings. Again, check

the list of ingredients as you would with dry foods.

On the topic of semi-moist dog foods, it is our opinion that these are not worth feeding to any dog. They don't have the advantages of either dry or canned foods and they have major disadvantages. Of primary concern are the additives used to keep the food "semi-moist," which by most accounts include a chemical that can be harmful to animals. In addition, the amount of sweeteners added makes the food highly desirable to dogs but very unhealthy overall. Fortunately, the cost of feeding semi-moist food to a Tosa is prohibitive so, on cost alone, you should spare your dog this poor food choice.

RAW-FOOD DIETS

There is a strong movement to raw-food diets for dogs. They consist of raw, hormone- and antibiotic-free meats with a small proportion of grains and vegetables. There has been much research that points to reduced incidences of cancer, arthritis, auto-immune illnesses and other debilitating diseases in dogs fed raw-food diets. However, in the cost and time categories, this diet is unrealistic for most dog owners. Some pre-packaged raw-food diets have recently become available. Due to their short shelf lives, they are usually made and distributed on a local or regional level. These

GRAIN-BASED DIETS

Some less expensive dog foods are based on grains and other plant proteins. While these products may appear to be attractively priced, breeders prefer a diet based on animal proteins and believe that they are more conducive to your dog's health. Many grain-based diets rely on soy protein, which may cause flatulence (passing gas).

There are many cases, however, when your dog might require a special diet. These special requirements should only be recommended by your veterinarian.

are more convenient for dog owners but may still be cost-prohibitive for feeding your large Tosa. However, a strong argument can be made that spending money on your dog's healthy diet may save you costly veterinary bills in the long run. This is where each individual owner must weigh the pros and cons of their feeding programs.

SUPPLEMENTS

Regarding supplements, there are also many opinions. Many vets and pet-food companies believe that if a dog is fed a "nutritionally complete and balanced diet," supplements would actually disrupt the balanced nutrition and be harmful. However, our 20 years of experience in breeding dogs

Your Tosa's diet is reflected in the dog's coat quality, musculature and behavior. Selecting the right food for your Tosa is one of the most important decisions you will make as an owner.

glucosamine and chondroiton, which have been proven to be effective in minimizing or reversing the symptoms of arthritis in humans. We have found them to be very effective in dogs with joint problems or older dogs with arthritis. Vitamin C is a strong antioxidant and another helpful supplement. Although dogs do make their own vitamin C, it is only about 40 mg per day, well below the recommended 1000–4000 mg per day that we find beneficial for the large- or giant-breed dogs.

A good multi-vitamin and mineral supplement is also beneficial. There has been noticeable

has led us to other conclusions. There are a few supplements that we consider essential to a dog's health, and others that we consider useful but not critical.

The essential supplements are digestive enzymes and probiotics. Naturally occurring enzymes and probiotics are largely destroyed during the high-temperature cooking required to make all processed dog foods. Enzymes assist in the stomach's digestive ability and probiotics encourage the growth of healthy bacteria in the intestines. Both supplements contribute to better, more complete digestion and assimilation of the nutrients in the Tosa's food.

Non-essential but helpful supplements include

CHANGE IN DIET

As your dog's caretaker, you know the importance of keeping his diet consistent, but sometimes when you run out of food or if you're on vacation, you have to make a change quickly. Some dogs will experience digestive problems, but most will not. If you are planning on changing your dog's menu, do so gradually to ensure that your dog will not have any problems. Over a period of five to seven days, slowly add some new food to your dog's old food, increasing the percentage of new food each day.

Proper diet and exercise are required to yield a healthy Tosa of the correct weight and structure. Soundness and good health are functions of the dog's breeding and then maintained by proper care.

of oil. However, a pup that cannot nurse should be watched closely because it will be at a double disadvantage: whatever caused the weakness in the first place compounded by not receiving the immune-boosting colostrum.

If a dam and her litter are all healthy, the puppies will nurse for four to six weeks and the dam

World Champion East West Riki, sharing a little unsolicited advice with her puppy.

differences in our dog's coat condition and overall health with the use of this type of supplement.

FEEDING FOR THE STAGES OF YOUR TOSA'S LIFE

Tosas, like all other dogs, receive all of their nutrition from their mother for the first few weeks of life. For the first one to three days, the dam produces a rich creamy colostrum, which plays an important role in strengthening the puppies' immune systems. It contains natural antibodies that provide puppies with immunity from many diseases for the first 10 to 16 weeks of life and helps create a well-functioning immune system for the life of the dog.

A puppy that is too sick or weak to suckle for the first few days can be tube-fed or bottle-fed under a vet's guidance. There are acceptable puppy formulas available, or your vet may recommend a home-made formula using goat's milk, egg yolk and a small amount

THE CANINE GOURMET

Your dog does not prefer a fresh bone. Indeed, he wants it properly aged and, if given such a treat indoors, he is more likely to try to bury it in the carpet than he is to settle in for a good chew! If you have a yard, give him such delicacies outside and guide him to a place suitable for his "bone yard." He will carefully place the treasure in its earthy vault and seemingly forget about it. Trust me, his seeming distaste or lack of thanks for your thoughtfulness is not that at all. He will return in a few days to inspect the bone, perhaps to re-bury it, and when it is just right, he will relish it as much as you do that cooked-to-perfection steak. If he is in a concrete or bricked kennel run, he will be especially frustrated at the hopelessness of the situation. He will vacillate between ignoring it completely, giving it a few licks to speed the curing process with saliva and trying to hide it behind the water bowl! When the bone has aged a bit, he will set to work on it.

Mother knows best, especially when she weighs over 175 pounds! DogStar's Queen Saba with her litter in Poland.

will naturally wean them. At about four weeks, the nutritional demands of the puppies become too great for the mother. At this time, breeders slowly introduce a smooth mixture of blended puppy kibble and goat's milk. By eight weeks, the pups will be fully weaned. Most of the time, the dam will take care of this herself by not letting the pups nurse, but sometimes the breeder may have to separate dam and pups for a few days so they don't bother her for milk. If the dam is still producing milk when separated from her pups, she will need special care to dry up her milk.

Gradually the pups will be able to eat firmer food and by eight weeks, when their puppy teeth have grown in, they should be eating a diet that consists primarily of puppy dry food. After weaning, it is advisable to feed the pups every six hours, four times per day. This gives them a consistent nutrient supply, which keeps their total systems, especially their immune systems, developing at optimal levels.

Due to the special growth demands of giant breeds like the Tosa, several companies have developed dry foods specifically designed for large-breed puppies. The ratio of ingredients is designed so that the puppies will grow more slowly, thus placing less stress on their bones, muscles and ligaments. Follow the feeding portions on the label and increase

HOW TO PREVENT BLOAT

Research has confirmed that the structure of deep-chested breeds contributes to their predisposition to bloat. Nevertheless, there are several precautions that you can take to reduce the risk of this condition:

• Feed your dog twice daily rather than offer one big meal.
• Do not exercise your dog for at least one hour before and two hours after he has eaten.
• Make certain that your dog is calm and not overly excited while he is eating. It has been proven that nervous or overly excited dogs are more prone to develop bloat.
• Add a small portion of moist meat product to his dry-food ration.
• Serve his meals in an elevated bowl stand, which avoids the dog's craning his neck while eating.
• To prevent your dog from gobbling his food too quickly, and thereby swallowing air, put some large (unswallowable) toys into his bowl so that he will have to eat around them to get his food.

the food as the puppy gains weight. Don't make the mistake of letting your Tosa free-feed or eat more than recommended. Allowing your puppy to become overweight causes too much stress on his bones and muscles. A healthy pup (after weaning) should be lean enough to see the outline of his ribs without his hip joints sticking out.

Keep your pup on puppy dry food designed for large-breed puppies until he is four to five months of age. At this time, reduce the feedings to three times per day and switch to adult dry food with supplementation. Most breeds will stay on puppy dry food until they are 18 months old, but this is not recommended for Tosas. By switching to an adult food, their growth is moderated

(not stunted) so that their bones, muscles and joints grow in unison.

Whenever you switch foods, do it slowly over the course of a week to avoid digestive upsets. Because dogs eat the same food every day, their systems cannot adapt to sudden changes in diet. At 8–12 months, switch your Tosa to two feedings per day, still feeding the same amount of food as recommended on the label, but divided into two meals. Adult Tosas should always be fed two times per day. If your Tosa is very active and needs more food than the amount recommended, be cautious about increasing the amount of food. You can vary the amount by one or two additional cups per day, but any more than that will cause digestive problems.

It is not required that all older dogs switch to senior diets. Some dogs do perfectly fine on adult food for their entire lives. If your older Tosa begins to gain weight, consider a senior-type food. They are bulkier so you can feed less and the dog will still feel full. Some dogs do not do well on senior food; loose stools, flatulence and low energy may be noticed. Feeding a smaller quantity of adult food or even puppy dry food may solve the problem. The Tosa is a very stoical breed and you will have to pay attention to your dog's changing needs as he ages in order to provide the optimal nutrition for your individual dog.

WATER

Fresh water is essential to your Tosa's health. Water keeps your dog's body hydrated and allows all systems to function normally. Change the water once or twice a day and keep the bowl elevated to chest level, just like when feeding. Give your dog the same quality water that you drink yourself. If you filter for chlorine or other contaminants, do the same for your dog. Clean the water bowl often. And beware— have a towel ready if you are near a Tosa who is drinking. A Tosa will often shake his head and shower you with fresh watery drool if you don't wipe his jowls first!

DRINK, DRANK, DRUNK— MAKE IT A DOUBLE

In both humans and dogs, as well as other living organisms, water forms the major part of nearly every body tissue. Naturally, we take water for granted, but without it, life as we know it would cease.

For dogs, water is needed to keep their bodies functioning biochemically. Additionally, water is needed to replace the water lost while panting. Unlike humans, who are able to sweat to dissipate heat, dogs must pant to cool down, thereby losing the vital water that their bodies need to regulate their body temperatures. Humans lose electrolyte-containing products and other body-fluid components through sweating; dogs do not lose anything except water.

Water is essential always, but especially so when the weather is hot or humid or when your dog is exercising or working vigorously.

EXERCISE FOR YOUR TOSA

All dogs require exercise for optimal health. Many people assume that, because of their size, Tosas require a lot of exercise; however, the Japanese bred for a dog with superior muscle tone who could live in the confined smaller areas available in that country, so the need for exercise is not proportionate to size. Tosas are very athletic and keep excellent muscle tone with a minimum of exercise. If a Tosa has a fenced yard, he will usually exercise himself as he patrols his territory. The Tosa will also play hard with another dog to keep himself in prime shape.

Tosas love exercise and thrive on long walks. In Japan, mature Tosas in top form are exercised on the beach. We don't recommend the larger Tosas for long-distance running, at least on streets or sidewalks. This is hard on their joints and may lead to premature joint problems. But average exercise—running or walking, playing or wrestling—is extremely beneficial for the Tosa.

During the formative stage, 4 to 18 months of age, it is best to refrain from excessively vigorous exercise, as a Tosa's bones, joints, ligaments and muscles are developing rapidly and are vulnerable to injury. Often a puppy's bones will grow faster than the ligaments and muscles, which creates stress on the joints. Gentle exercise will strengthen muscles without causing injury.

Some breeders and trainers don't recommend playing tug-of-war with your Tosa. However, we have found it to be a stimulating activity for both dog and human if done correctly. Start your dog young and play gently, especially while your puppy is getting his adult teeth (four to six months of age). Let the pup win sometimes to build his confidence. When you play tug-of-war with a Tosa pup, make sure he understands that this is play. The first thing you must do is to teach him the "out" command so he will drop the tug toy on command. Discontinue the game if your dog gets too worked up; this is the time for a cool-down period.

EXERCISE ALERT!
You should be careful where you exercise your dog. Many areas have been sprayed with chemicals that are highly toxic to both dogs and humans. Never allow your dog to eat grass or drink from puddles on either public or private grounds, as the run-off water may contain chemicals from sprays and herbicides.

Since they were bred as fighting dogs, Tosas have a natural desire to wrestle as puppies. They will wrestle and bite and that is completely natural. Let them explore their physical range with their littermates but do not let the biting behavior occur between you and the pup. Even at this age, your puppy can learn to distinguish what types of behavior is appropriate and with whom.

Most Tosas don't play fetch naturally like retrievers, collies or spaniels. A few may use their strong prey drive to make the "fetch" into a wonderful game. Again be sure your Tosa knows that this is a game and not about possession of the toy. Your Tosa should let you reach for the toy or ball without any hint of possessiveness. Work with your pup so that he knows that he should not guard the toy possessively or show any aggression if someone attempts to take it away.

GROOMING

The Tosa is a wonderfully easy dog to groom because of his short coat. Periodic brushing with a natural bristle brush in the direction of the coat will remove loose hair and debris. Some Tosas develop a winter undercoat that sheds out in the spring. We find it helpful to use a horse shedding blade to remove the longer, finer winter coat. Tosas don't shed a lot under normal circumstances, so if

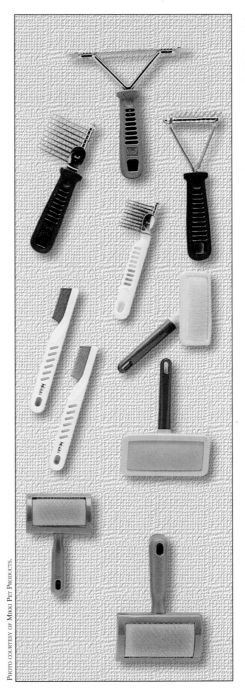

PHOTO COURTESY OF MIKKI PET PRODUCTS.

Tosas require little grooming, but periodic brushing does remove dead hair. You should be able to find what you need for grooming your Tosa where you buy pet supplies.

Special shedding blades are often used to remove the dead hairs of the winter coat when needed.

More usual is the use of a natural bristle brush. The wire bristle side may also be used to remove foreign matter from the dog's coat.

While bathing is rarely necessary, special shampoo made for dogs should be used whenever the need arises.

SKUNK REMEDY

If your Tosa has the misfortune of being sprayed by a skunk, a quick and thorough cleaning is required. There are commercial skunk-odor-removal preparations, or make one quickly at home, using 2 quarts of 3% hydrogen peroxide, one-half cup of baking soda and 2 tablespoons of liquid dish detergent. Apply to a dry coat, making sure that the entire coat is wet. Use a sponge or cloth for the face so that you can avoid the eyes. Let stand for a few minutes and rinse completely. Reapply if needed.

you notice unusual amounts of shedding, it may be a sign of allergies, skin conditions or illness, or even a need for essential fatty-acid supplementation.

Tosas are very clean, so frequent bathing is not necessary. However when it is bath time for your Tosa, you will have a difficult time getting him into a bathtub due to his large size. To get warm water for an outside bath, try hooking up a hose bib to your house sink. Use mild dog shampoo; human shampoos are not recommended for dogs due to different pH balances, although you may use a "no-tear" baby shampoo for the face. Always rinse your Tosa thoroughly.

Many Tosas are outside dogs and their nails are kept short as a result of their natural outdoor activities. However, if your Tosa needs to have his nails clipped, get the best, largest and sharpest guillotine-type clipper you can. Tosas' nails are very thick and it is difficult to get a clean cut. Quite honestly, we have found that having the veterinarian clip the nails during a regular health check-up is the best option.

Clean your Tosa's ears periodically. Be alert for signs of infection like shaking of the head or unpleasant odor. Use a prepared ear solution or make one of equal parts water, mineral oil and rubbing alcohol. Use a cotton ball or swab to gently clean the inside of the ear. Only clean the part of the ear you can see. Inserting a cotton swab further into the ear may cause damage.

Tosas, due to their heavy weight, may get calluses on their

Be sure to remove all of the shampoo from the dog's coat once it has been applied. Residue left in the dog's coat can be irritating.

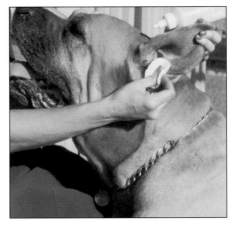

Left: The ears should be cleaned with a soft wipe. Use an ear-cleaning solution to remove any accumulated dirt or ear wax.

Below: A cooperative Tosa receiving his pedicure.

PEDICURE TIP

A dog that spends a lot of time outside on a hard surface, such as cement or pavement, will have his nails naturally worn down and may not need to have them trimmed as often, except maybe in the colder months when he is not outside as much. Regardless, it is best to get your dog accustomed to the nail-trimming procedure at an early age so that he is used to it. Some dogs are especially sensitive about having their feet touched, but if a dog has experienced it since puppyhood, it should not bother him.

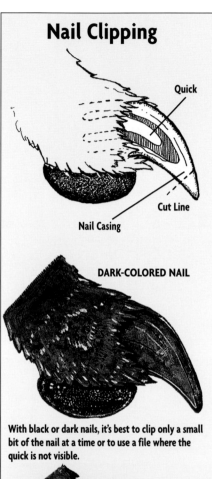

Nail Clipping

Quick

Cut Line

Nail Casing

DARK-COLORED NAIL

With black or dark nails, it's best to clip only a small bit of the nail at a time or to use a file where the quick is not visible.

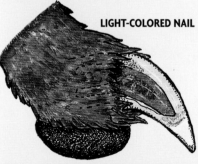

LIGHT-COLORED NAIL

In light-colored nails, clipping is simpler because you can see the vein (or quick) that grows inside the casing. Most Tosas, however, have dark nails.

THE WEEKLY GRIND

You can purchase an electric tool to grind down a dog's nails rather than cut them. Some dogs don't seem to mind the electric grinder but will object strongly to nail clippers. If your Tosa reacts poorly to the clippers, give the grinder a try.

hips and elbows. Use a thick foam-pad carpeting or other soft bedding to prevent this condition. If your Tosa develops calluses, use a balm, petroleum jelly or other emollient ointments to soften and prevent cracking and possible bleeding.

TRAVELING WITH YOUR DOG

CAR TRAVEL

You should accustom your Tosa to riding in a car at an early age. You may or may not take him in the car often, but at the very least he will need to go to the vet and you do not want these trips to be traumatic for the dog or troublesome for you. The safest way for a dog to ride in the car is in his crate, provided you have a vehicle that can accommodate your Tosa's very large crate.

Put the pup in the crate and see how he reacts. If he seems uneasy, you can have a passenger hold him on his lap while you drive. Another option for car travel is a specially made safety harness for dogs, which straps the dog in much like a seat belt. With sport utility or similar vehicles, you can partition the back section of the vehicle to give your dog a safe area. Whichever option you choose, do not let the dog roam loose in the vehicle—this is very dangerous! If you should stop short, your dog can be thrown and injured. If the dog starts climbing on you and pestering you while you are driving, you will not be able to concentrate on the road. It is an unsafe situation for everyone—human and canine.

For long trips, be prepared to stop to let the dog relieve himself. Take with you whatever you need to clean up after him, including some paper towels and perhaps some old rags for use should he have a potty accident in the car or suffer from motion sickness.

AIR TRAVEL

Contact your chosen airline before proceeding with your travel plans that include your Tosa. The dog will be required to travel in a fiberglass crate and you should always check in advance with the airline regarding specific requirements for the crate's size, type and labeling. To help put the dog at ease, give him one of his favorite toys in the crate. Do not feed the dog for several hours prior to checking in so that you minimize his need to relieve himself. Some airlines require you to provide documentation as to when the dog has last been fed. In any case, a light meal is best. For long trips, you will have to attach food and water bowls and a portion of food to the dog's crate so that airline employees can tend to him between legs of the trip.

Make sure your dog is properly identified and that your contact information appears on his ID tags and on his crate. Your

TRAVEL TIP
The most extensive travel you do with your dog may be limited to trips to the vet's office—or you may decide to bring him along for long distances when the family goes on vacation. Whichever the case, it is important to consider your dog's safety while traveling.

Tosa will travel in a different area of the plane than the human passengers, so every rule must be strictly followed to prevent the slight risk of getting separated from your dog.

BOARDING AND VACATIONS

So you want to take a family vacation—and you want to include *all* members of the family. You would probably make arrangements for accommodations ahead of time anyway, but this is especially important when traveling with a dog. You do not want to make an

overnight stop at the only place around for miles, only to find out that they do not allow dogs. Also, you do not want to reserve a place for your family without confirming that you are traveling with a dog, because, if it is against the hotel's policy, you may end up without a place to stay.

Alternatively, if you are traveling and choose not to bring your Tosa, you will have to make arrangements for him while you are away. Some options are to take him to a neighbor's house to stay while you are gone, to have a

IDENTIFICATION OPTIONS

As puppies become more and more expensive, especially those puppies of high quality for showing and/or breeding, they have a greater chance of being stolen. The usual collar dog tag is, of course, easily removed. But there are two more permanent techniques that have become widely used for identifying dogs.

The puppy microchip implantation involves the injection of a small microchip, about the size of a corn kernel, under the skin of the dog. If your dog shows up at a clinic or shelter, or is offered for resale under less-than-savory circumstances, it can be positively identified by the microchip. The microchip is scanned, and a registry quickly identifies you as the owner.

Tattooing is done on various parts of the dog, from his belly to his ears. The number tattooed can be your telephone number, the dog's registration number or any other number that you can easily memorize. When professional dog thieves see a tattooed dog, they usually lose interest. For the safety of our dogs, no laboratory facility or dog broker will accept a tattooed dog as stock.

Discuss microchipping and tattooing with your vet and breeder. Some vets perform these services on their own premises for a reasonable fee. To ensure that the dog's ID is effective, be certain that the dog is then properly registered with a legitimate national database.

trusted neighbor stay at your house and watch him or to bring your dog to a reputable boarding kennel. If you choose to board him at a kennel, you should visit in advance to see the facilities provided and where the dogs are kept. Are the dogs' areas spacious and kept clean? Talk to some of the employees and see how they treat the dogs—have they experience with giant breeds; do they spend time with the dogs, play with them, exercise them, etc.? Also find out the kennel's policy on vaccinations and what they require. This is for all of the dogs' safety, since there is a greater risk of diseases being passed from dog to dog when dogs are kept together.

IDENTIFICATION

Your Tosa is your valued companion and friend. That is why you always keep a close eye on him and you have made sure that he cannot escape from the yard or wriggle out of his collar and run away from you. However, accidents can happen and there may come a time when your dog unexpectedly becomes separated from you. If this unfortunate event should occur, the first thing on your mind will be finding him. Proper identification, including an ID tag, and possibly a tattoo and/or microchip, will increase the chances of his being returned to you safely and quickly.

When training a dog as large as a Tosa, it's prudent to understand how this headstrong Japanese canine thinks.

TRAINING YOUR

JAPANESE TOSA

The Tosa is known for being a very intelligent breed. The breed's background in the fighting ring required dogs that could listen and respond to verbal commands while in the ring. The Tosa's ability to respond to human commands has been reinforced by the Japanese breeding programs.

The Tosa will work very hard to understand what you mean and wants very much to please you by doing the right thing. This intelligence has some drawbacks. One is that a Tosa will get bored with repetitive training methods. A Tosa learns quickly and, if asked to do the same thing over and over, a Tosa may get bored and do something to liven up the training session. This may lead to the impression that Tosas are stubborn or don't learn well, but if you recognize this as a sign of their quick learning capabilities, you will be able to come up with creative ways to engage your Tosa. Make the training stimulating and not just boring repetitions (remember the multiplication tables you had to memorize?).

Another drawback to working with Tosas occurs when the human (or humans) gives conflicting or inconsistent commands. A Tosa will try hard to figure out what is being asked, but, if it is not clear, he may divert his attention to other things. Again this could be interpreted as stubbornness, but it is usually a need for greater concentration and clarity on the part of the trainer.

Training cannot be done once and expected to hold for life. Work with your Tosa often, daily if possible. Run through the basic commands; this keeps your Tosa mentally alert, gives him attention and provides a great opportunity for fun. Make it enjoyable for your Tosa and he will make it enjoyable for you!

To train your Tosa, you may like to enroll in an obedience class. Teach your dog good manners as you learn how and why he behaves the way he does. Find out how to communicate with your dog and how to recognize and understand his communications with you. Suddenly the dog takes on a new role in your life—he is clever, interesting, well behaved and fun to be with. He demonstrates his bond of devotion to you daily. In other words, your Tosa does wonders for your ego because he constantly reminds you that you are not only his leader, you are his hero!

Those involved with teaching dog obedience and counseling owners about their dogs' behavior have discovered some interesting facts about dog ownership. For example, training dogs when they are puppies results in the highest rate of success in developing well-mannered and well-adjusted adult dogs. Training an older dog, from six months to six years of age, can produce almost equal results, providing that the owner accepts the dog's slower rate of learning capability and is willing to work patiently to help the dog succeed at developing to his fullest potential. Unfortunately, many owners of untrained adult dogs lack the patience factor, so they do not persist until their dogs are successful at learning particular behaviors.

Training a puppy aged 10 to 16 weeks (20 weeks at the most) is like working with a dry sponge in a pool of water. The pup soaks up whatever you show him and constantly looks for more things to do and learn. At this early age, his body is not yet producing hormones, and therein lies the reason for such a high rate of success. Without hormones, he is focused on his owners and not particularly

> **REAP THE REWARDS**
>
> If you start with a normal, healthy dog and give him time, patience and some carefully executed lessons, you will reap the rewards of that training for the life of the dog. And what a life it will be! The two of you will find immeasurable pleasure in the companionship you have built together with love, respect and understanding.

interested in investigating other places, dogs, people, etc. You are his leader: his provider of food, water, shelter and security. He latches onto you and wants to stay close. He will usually follow you from room to room, will not let you out of his sight when you are outdoors with him and will respond in like manner to the people and animals you encounter. If you greet a friend warmly, he will be happy to greet the person as well. If, however, you are hesitant or anxious about the approach of a stranger, he will respond accordingly.

Once the puppy begins to produce hormones, his natural curiosity emerges and he begins to investigate the world around him. It is at this time when you may notice that the untrained dog begins to wander away from you and even ignore your commands to stay close. When this behavior becomes a problem, you have two choices: get rid of the dog or train him. It is strongly urged that you choose the latter option.

You usually will be able to find obedience classes within a reasonable distance from your home, but you can also do a lot to train your dog yourself. Sometimes there are classes available, but the tuition is too costly. Whatever the circumstances, the solution to training your dog without obedience classes lies within the pages of this book.

This chapter is devoted to helping you train your Tosa at home. If the recommended procedures are followed faithfully, you may expect positive results that will prove rewarding both to you and your dog.

Whether your new charge is a puppy or a mature adult, the methods of teaching and the techniques we use in training basic behaviors are the same. After all, no dog, whether puppy or adult, likes harsh or inhumane methods. All creatures, however, respond favorably to gentle motivational methods and sincere praise and encouragement. Now let us get started.

HOUSE-TRAINING
You can train a puppy to relieve himself wherever you choose, but this must be somewhere suitable. You should bear in mind

from the outset that when your puppy is old enough to go out in public places, any canine deposits must be removed at once. You will always have to carry with you a small plastic bag or "poop-scoop."

Outdoor training includes such surfaces as grass, soil and cement. Indoor training usually means training your dog to newspaper, not a viable option with a giant breed like the Tosa. When deciding on the surface and location that you will want your Tosa to use, be sure it is going to be permanent. Training your dog to grass and then changing your

A characteristic of all puppies is curiosity. You must start training your Tosa before the urge to explore becomes the focus of his attention.

PAPER CAPER

Never line your pup's sleeping area with newspaper. Puppy litters are usually raised on newspaper and, once in your home, the puppy will immediately associate newspaper with voiding. Never put newspaper on any floor while house-training, as this will only confuse the puppy, and the Tosa is certainly too large to paper-train. Finally, restrict water intake after evening meals. Offer a few licks at a time—never let a Tosa of any age gulp water after meals.

mind a few months later is extremely difficult for both dog and owner.

Next, choose the command you will use each and every time you want your puppy to void. "Hurry up" and "Toilet" are examples of commands commonly used by dog owners. Get in the habit of giving the puppy your chosen relief command before you take him out. That way, when he becomes an adult, you will be able to determine if he wants to go out when you ask him. A confirmation will be signs of interest, such as wagging his tail, watching you intently, going to the door, etc.

PUPPY'S NEEDS

The puppy needs to relieve himself after play periods, after each meal, after he has been sleeping and at any time he indicates that he is looking for a place to urinate or defecate. The urinary and intestinal tract muscles of very young puppies are not fully developed. Therefore, like human babies, puppies need to relieve themselves frequently.

Take your puppy out often—every hour for an eight-week-old, for example—and always immediately after sleeping and eating. The older the puppy, the less often he will need to relieve himself. Finally, as a mature healthy adult, he will require only three to five relief trips per day.

CANINE DEVELOPMENT SCHEDULE

It is important to understand how and at what age a puppy develops into adulthood. If you are a puppy owner, consult the following Canine Development Schedule to determine the stage of development your puppy is currently experiencing. This knowledge will help you as you work with the puppy in the weeks and months ahead.

Period	Age	Characteristics
FIRST TO THIRD	**BIRTH TO SEVEN WEEKS**	Puppy needs food, sleep and warmth, and responds to simple and gentle touching. Needs mother for security and disciplining. Needs littermates for learning and interacting with other dogs. Pup learns to function within a pack and learns pack order of dominance. Begin socializing pup with adults and children for short periods. Pup begins to become aware of his environment.
FOURTH	**EIGHT TO TWELVE WEEKS**	Brain is fully developed. Needs socializing with outside world. Remove from mother and littermates. Needs to change from canine pack to human pack. Human dominance necessary. Fear period occurs between 8 and 12 weeks. Avoid fright and pain.
FIFTH	**THIRTEEN TO SIXTEEN WEEKS**	Training and formal obedience should begin. Less association with other dogs, more with people, places, situations. Period will pass easily if you remember this is pup's change-to-adolescence time. Be firm and fair. Flight instinct prominent. Permissiveness and over-disciplining can do permanent damage. Praise for good behavior.
JUVENILE	**FOUR TO EIGHT MONTHS**	Another fear period about 7 to 8 months of age. It passes quickly, but be cautious of fright and pain. Sexual maturity reached. Dominant traits established. Dog should understand sit, down, come and stay by now.

NOTE: THESE ARE APPROXIMATE TIME FRAMES. ALLOW FOR INDIVIDUAL DIFFERENCES IN PUPPIES.

PARENTAL GUIDANCE

Training a dog is a life experience. Many parents admit that much of what they know about raising children they learned from caring for their dogs. Dogs respond to love, fairness and guidance, just as children do. Become a good dog owner and you may become an even better parent.

HOUSING

Since the types of housing and control you provide for your puppy have a direct relationship on the success of house-training, we consider the various aspects of both before we begin training. Taking a new puppy home and turning him loose in your house can be compared to turning a child loose in a sports arena and telling the child that the place is all his! The sheer enormity of the place would be too much for him to handle. Instead, offer the puppy clearly defined areas where he can play, sleep, eat and live. A room of the house where the family gathers is the most obvious choice. Puppies are social animals and need to feel a part of the pack right from the start. Hearing your voice, watching you while you are doing things and smelling you nearby are all positive reinforcers that he is now a member of your pack. Usually a family room, the kitchen or a nearby adjoining breakfast area is ideal for providing safety and security for both puppy and owner.

Within the designated room, there should be a smaller area that the puppy can call his own. An alcove, a wire or fiberglass dog crate or a gated (not boarded!) corner from which he can view the activities of his new family will be fine. The size of the area or crate is the key factor here. The area must be large enough so that the puppy can lie down and stretch out, as well as stand up, without rubbing his head on the top. At the same time, it must be small enough so that he cannot relieve himself at one end and sleep at the other without coming into contact with his droppings before he is fully trained to relieve himself outside. Dogs are, by nature, clean animals and will not remain close to their relief areas unless forced to do so. In those cases, they then become dirty dogs and usually remain that way for life.

The dog's designated area should contain clean bedding and a toy. Water must always be available, in a non-spill container, once house-training has been achieved reliably.

CONTROL

By *control*, we mean helping the puppy to create a lifestyle pattern that will be compatible to that of his human pack *(you!)*. Just as we guide little children to learn our way of life, we must show the puppy when it is time to play, eat, sleep, exercise and even entertain himself.

Your puppy should always sleep in his crate. He should also learn that, during times of household confusion and excessive human activity, such as at breakfast when family members are preparing for the day, he can play by himself in relative safety and comfort in his designated area. Each time you leave the puppy alone, he should understand exactly where he is to stay.

Puppies are chewers. They cannot tell the difference between lamp cords, television wires, shoes, table legs, etc. Chewing into a television wire, for example, can be fatal to the puppy, while a shorted wire can start a fire in the house. If the puppy chews on the arm of the chair when he is alone, you will probably discipline him angrily when you get home. Thus, he makes the association that your coming home means he is going to be punished. (He will not remember chewing the chair and is incapable of making the association of the discipline with his naughty deed.) Accustoming the pup to his designated area not only keeps him safe but also avoids his engaging in destructive behaviors when you are not around.

Times of excitement, such as special occasions, family parties,

CALM DOWN

Dogs will do anything for your attention. If you reward the dog when he is calm and resting, you will develop a well-mannered dog. If, on the other hand, you greet your dog excitedly and encourage him to wrestle with you, the dog will greet you the same way and you will have a hyperactive dog on your hands.

etc., can be fun for the puppy, providing that he can view the activities from the security of his designated area. He is not underfoot and he is not being fed all sorts of tidbits that will probably cause him stomach distress, yet he still feels a part of the fun.

SCHEDULE

A puppy should be taken to his relief area each time he is released from his designated area, after meals, after play sessions and when he first awakens in the morning (at age eight weeks, this can mean 5 a.m.!). The puppy will

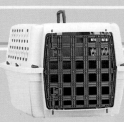

THE SUCCESS METHOD

Success that comes by luck is usually short-lived. Success that comes by well-thought-out proven methods is often more easily achieved and permanent. This is the Success Method. It is designed to give you, the puppy owner, a simple yet proven way to help your puppy develop clean living habits and a feeling of security in his new environment.

6 Steps to Successful Crate Training

1 Tell the puppy "Crate time!" and place him in the crate with a small treat (a piece of cheese or half of a biscuit). Let him stay in the crate for five minutes while you are in the same room. Then release him and praise lavishly. Never release him when he is fussing. Wait until he is quiet before you let him out.

2 Repeat Step 1 several times a day.

3 The next day, place the puppy in the crate as before. Let him stay there for ten minutes. Do this several times.

4 Continue building time in five-minute increments until the puppy stays in his crate for 30 minutes with you in the room. Always take him to his relief area after prolonged periods in his crate.

5 Now go back to Step 1 and let the puppy stay in his crate for five minutes, this time while you are out of the room.

6 Once again, build crate time in five-minute increments with you out of the room. When the puppy will stay willingly in his crate (he may even fall asleep!) for 30 minutes with you out of the room, he will be ready to stay in it for several hours at a time.

indicate that he's ready "to go" by circling or sniffing busily—do not misinterpret these signs. For a puppy less than ten weeks of age, a routine of taking him out every hour is necessary. As the puppy grows, he will be able to wait for longer periods of time.

Keep trips to his relief area short. Stay no more than five or six minutes and then return to the house. If he goes during that time, praise him lavishly and take him indoors immediately. If he does not, but he has an accident when you go back indoors, pick him up immediately, say "No! No!" and return to his relief area. Wait a few minutes, then return to the house again. Never hit a puppy or put his face in urine or excrement when he has had an accident!

Once indoors, put the puppy in his crate until you have had time to clean up his accident. Then, release him to the family area and watch him more closely than before. Chances are, his accident was a result of your not picking up his signal or waiting too long before offering him the opportunity to relieve himself. Never hold a grudge against the puppy for accidents.

Let the puppy learn that going outdoors means it is time to relieve himself, not to play. Once trained, he will be able to play indoors and out and still differentiate between the times for play versus the times for relief.

Help him develop regular hours for naps, being alone, playing by himself and just resting, all in his crate. Encourage him to entertain himself while you are busy with your activities. Let him learn that having you near is comforting, but it is not your main purpose in life to provide him with undivided attention.

Each time you put your puppy

When you understand how your Tosa thinks and train him accordingly, you'll find that he makes a bright, attentive student.

in his own area, use the same command, whatever suits best. Soon he will run to his crate or special area when he hears you say those words.

Crate training provides safety for you, the puppy and the home. It also provides the puppy with a feeling of security, and that helps the puppy achieve self-confidence and clean habits. Remember that one of the primary ingredients in house-training your puppy is control. Regardless of your lifestyle, there will always be occasions when you will need to have a place where your dog can stay and be happy and safe. Crate training is the answer for now and in the future.

In conclusion, a few key elements are really all you need for a successful house-training method—consistency, frequency, praise, control and supervision. By following these procedures with a normal, healthy puppy, you and the puppy will soon be past the stage of "accidents" and ready to move on to a full and rewarding life together.

ROLES OF DISCIPLINE, REWARD AND PUNISHMENT

Discipline, training one to act in accordance with rules, brings order to life. It is as simple as that. Without discipline, particularly in a group society, chaos will reign supreme and the group will eventually perish. Humans and

HOW MANY TIMES A DAY?	
AGE	RELIEF TRIPS
To 14 weeks	10
14–22 weeks	8
22–32 weeks	6
Adulthood	4
(dog stops growing)	

These are estimates, of course, but they are a guide to the *minimum* number of opportunities a dog should have each day to relieve himself.

canines are social animals and need some form of discipline in order to function effectively. They must procure food, reproduce to keep their species going and protect their home base and their young. If there were no discipline in the lives of social animals, they would eventually die from starvation and/or predation by other stronger animals. In the case of domestic canines, discipline in their lives is needed in order for them to understand how their pack (you and other family members) functions and how they must act in order to survive.

A large humane society in a highly populated area recently surveyed dog owners regarding their satisfaction with their relationships with their dogs. People who had trained their dogs were 75% more satisfied with their pets than those who had never trained their dogs.

Dr. Edward Thorndike, a noted psychologist, established *Thorndike's Theory of Learning*, which states that a behavior that results in a pleasant event tends to be repeated. A behavior that results in an unpleasant event tends not to be repeated. It is this theory upon which training methods are based today. For example, if you manipulate a dog to perform a specific behavior and reward him for doing it, he is likely to do it again because he enjoyed the end result.

Occasionally, punishment, a penalty inflicted for an offense, is necessary. The best type of punishment often comes from an outside source. For example, a child is told not to touch the stove because he may get burned. He disobeys and touches the stove. In doing so, he receives a burn. From that time on, he respects the heat of the stove and avoids contact with it. Therefore, a behavior that results in an unpleasant event tends not to be repeated.

A good example of a dog learning the hard way is the dog who chases the house cat. He is told many times to leave the cat alone, yet he persists in teasing the cat. Then, one day, the dog begins chasing the cat but the cat turns and swipes a claw across the dog's face, leaving the dog with a painful gash on his nose. The final result is that the dog stops chasing the cat. Again, a

behavior that results in an unpleasant event tends not to be repeated.

TRAINING EQUIPMENT

COLLAR AND LEASH
For a Tosa, the collar and leash that you use for training must be one with which you are easily able to work, not too heavy for the dog and perfectly safe.

TREATS
Have a bag of treats on hand; something nutritious and easy to swallow works best. Use a soft treat, a chunk of cheese or a piece

Keeping your Tosa's attention through the lesson is the key to succeeding at teaching the basic obedience commands. A tasty treat never hurts to keep your dog's focus.

Don't be afraid to let your Tosa know that you are the boss, even if he resembles the "king of the jungle" atop his stony perch.

of cooked chicken rather than a dry biscuit. By the time the puppy has finished chewing a dry treat, he will forget why he is being rewarded in the first place!

Using food rewards will not teach a dog to beg at the table— the only way to teach a dog to beg at the table is to give him food from the table. In training, rewarding the dog with a food treat will help him associate praise and the treats with learning new behaviors that obviously please his owner.

TOSA TRAINING TIPS
Tosas are very sensitive and respond well to light-handed training using food motivation. We recommend that you find a trainer who focuses on positive-reinforcement training and use this approach in working with your Tosa. These dogs understand your intentions quickly and can be easily trained. (Most training problems are with the owner, not

the dog.) Still, you need to stay consistent with your commands. You should speak firmly, without being heavy-handed because of the breed's sensitive nature.

Training the Tosa is best done with affection. Don't be soft with your Tosa; it is best if he knows that you are the pack leader from the beginning and that you act consistently. This allows the Tosa to reach his maximum potential as your family guard and companion. As he grows, you want to guide him in knowing what you expect of him. When you have earned his respect by understanding your role, he will want to do whatever you want. He looks to you for guidance. If you don't provide it, he will. Training can help you and your Tosa achieve a truly great relationship. It allows him to express his potential, while doing what you want him to do. Don't spoil him or impose human characteristics on him. This is a big mistake with a large, strong dog and can be hard to rehabilitate.

TRAINING BEGINS: ASK THE DOG A QUESTION
In order to teach your dog anything, you must first get his attention. After all, he cannot learn anything if he is looking away from you with his mind on something else.

To get your dog's attention, ask him "School?" and immedi-

TRAINING IS A "CLICK"

A fairly new method of training, clicker training, uses the sound of the "clicker" as a positive reinforcement for training purposes. The clicker is a small hand-held device that you press when the dog does something correct. It is used instead of or in conjunction with training with food motivation. Many Tosas trainers have had excellent results with this method.

means doing great things with you that are fun and that result in positive attention for him.

Remember that the dog does not understand your verbal language; he only recognizes sounds. Your question translates to a series of sounds for him, and those sounds become the signal to go to you and pay attention. The dog learns that if he does this, he will get to interact with you plus receive treats and praise.

Show handlers may not teach their dogs the sit command first, as the stand and stay commands are more apropos to the needs of the show ring.

ately walk over to him and give him a treat as you tell him "Good dog." Wait a minute or two and repeat the routine, this time with a treat in your hand as you approach within a foot of the dog. Do not go directly to him, but stop about a foot short of him and hold out the treat as you ask "School?" He will see you approaching with a treat in your hand and most likely begin walking toward you. As you meet, give him the treat and praise again.

The third time, ask the question, have a treat in your hand and walk only a short distance toward the dog so that he must walk almost all the way to you. As he reaches you, give him the treat and praise again.

By this time, the dog will probably be getting the idea that if he pays attention to you, especially when you ask that question, it will pay off in treats and enjoyable activities for him. In other words, he learns that "school"

THE BASIC COMMANDS

TEACHING SIT

Now that you have the dog's attention, attach his leash and hold it in your left hand, and hold a food treat in your right hand. Place your food hand at the dog's nose and let him lick the treat but not take it from you. Say "Sit" and slowly raise your food hand from in front of the dog's nose up over his head so that he is looking at the ceiling. As he bends his head upward, he will have to bend his knees to maintain his balance. As he bends his knees,

Having your Tosa sit politely during grooming is just one of the practical benefits of teaching the command. Imagine how difficult it would be to do simple tasks with a large dog if he were not trained!

he will assume a sit position. At that point, release the food treat and praise lavishly with comments such as "Good dog! Good sit!" Remember to always praise enthusiastically, because dogs relish verbal praise from their owners and feel so proud of themselves whenever they accomplish a behavior.

You will not use food forever in getting the dog to obey your commands. Food is only used to teach new behaviors and, once the dog knows what you want when you give a specific command, you will wean him off the food treats but still maintain the verbal praise. After all, you will always have your voice with you, and there will be many times when you have no food rewards but expect the dog to obey.

TEACHING DOWN

Because the Tosa is a strong-minded, dominant breed, at times we have had difficulty with the down command as this is a submissive position for a dog. Our solution has been to begin early and to make it fun for the Tosa. By giving our Tosas praise while they are in the down position and making it into a game, we have had more success with this exercise.

Teaching the down exercise is much easier when you understand how the dog perceives the down position, and it is much more difficult when you do not. Since dogs perceive the down position as a submissive one, teaching the down exercise by using a forceful method can sometimes make the dog develop such a fear of the down that he either runs away when you say "Down" or he attempts to snap at the person who tries to force him down.

Have the dog sit close along-side your left leg, facing in the same direction as you are. Hold the leash in your left hand and a food treat in your right. Now place your left hand lightly on the top of the dog's shoulders where they meet above the spinal cord. Do not push down on the dog's shoulders; simply rest your left hand there so you can guide the dog to lie down close to your left leg rather than to swing away from your side when he drops.

Now place the food hand at the dog's nose, say "Down" very softly (almost a whisper) and slowly lower the food hand to the dog's front feet. When the food hand reaches the floor, begin moving it forward along the floor in front of the dog. Keep talking softly to the dog, saying things like, "Do you want this treat? You can do this, good dog." Your reas-suring tone of voice will help calm the dog as he tries to follow the food hand in order to get the treat.

When the dog's elbows touch the floor, release the food and praise softly. Try to get the dog to maintain that down position for several seconds before you let him sit up again. The goal here is to get the dog to settle down and not feel threatened in the down position.

TEACHING STAY

It is easy to teach the dog to stay in either a sit or a down position. Again, we use food and praise during the teaching process as we help the dog to understand exactly what it is that we are expecting him to do.

DOUBLE JEOPARDY

A dog in jeopardy never lies down. He stays alert on his feet because instinct tells him that he may have to run away or fight for his survival. Therefore, if a dog feels threatened or anxious, he will not lie down. Consequently, it is important to keep the dog calm and relaxed as he learns the down exercise.

To teach the sit/stay, start with the dog sitting on your left side as before and hold the leash in your left hand. Have a food treat in your right hand and place your food hand at the dog's nose. Say "Stay" and step out on your right foot to stand directly in front of the dog, toe to toe, as he licks and nibbles the treat. Be sure to keep his head facing upward to maintain the sit position. Count to five and then swing around to stand next to the dog again with him on your left. As soon as you get back to the original position, release the food and praise lavishly.

Good manners run in the family. Posing are World Champion Ryoma with his daughter East West Tayoma, owned by DogStar Kennels.

CONSISTENCY PAYS OFF

Dogs need consistency in their feeding schedule, exercise and relief visits, and in the verbal commands you use. If you use "Stay" on Monday and "Stay here, please" on Tuesday, you will confuse your dog. Don't demand perfect behavior during training sessions and then let him have the run of the house the rest of the day. Above all, lavish praise on your pet consistently every time he does something right. The more he feels he is pleasing you, the more willing he will be to learn.

To teach the down/stay, do the down as previously described. As soon as the dog lies down, say "Stay" and step out on your right foot just as you did in the sit/stay. Count to five and then return to stand beside the dog with him on your left side. Release the treat and praise as always.

Within a week or ten days, you can begin to add a bit of distance between you and your dog when you leave him. When you do, use your left hand open with the palm facing the dog as a stay signal, much the same as the hand signal a police officer uses to stop traffic at an intersection. Hold the food treat in your right hand as before, but this time the food will not be touching the dog's nose. He will watch the food hand and quickly learn that he is going to get that treat as soon as you return to his side.

When you can stand 3 feet away from your dog for 30 seconds, you can then begin building time and distance in both stays. Eventually, the dog can be expected to remain in the stay position for prolonged periods of time until you return to him or call him to you. Always praise lavishly when he stays.

Teaching Come

If you make teaching "come" an exciting experience, you should never have a "student" that does not love the game or that fails to come when called. The secret, it seems, is never to teach the word "come."

At times when an owner most wants his dog to come when called, the owner is likely to be upset or anxious and he allows these feelings to come through in the tone of his voice when he calls his dog. Hearing that desperation in his owner's voice, the dog fears the results of going to him and therefore either disobeys outright or runs in the opposite direction. The secret, therefore, is to teach the dog a game and, when you want him to come to you, simply play the game. It is practically a no-fail solution!

To begin, have several members of your family take a few food treats and each go into a different room in the house. Everyone takes turns calling the dog, and each person should celebrate the dog's finding him with a treat and lots of happy praise.

"WHERE ARE YOU?"
When calling the dog, do not say "Come." Say things like, "Rover, where are you? See if you can find me! I have a biscuit for you!" Keep up a constant line of chatter with coaxing sounds and frequent questions such as, "Where are you?" The dog will learn to follow the sound of your voice to locate you and receive his reward.

DogStar's Yama, illustrating a confident, well-educated student. (Who's going to argue?)

dogs will race to respond to a person who uses the dog's name followed by "Where are you?" For example, a woman has a 12-year-old companion dog who went blind, but who never fails to locate her owner when asked, "Where are you?"

Children, in particular, love to play this game with their dogs. Children can hide in smaller places like a shower or bathtub, behind a bed or under a table. The dog needs to work a little bit harder to find these hiding places, but, when he does, he loves to celebrate with a treat and a tussle with a favorite youngster.

When a person calls the dog, he is actually inviting the dog to find him and to get a treat as a reward for "winning."

A few turns of the "Where are you?" game and the dog will understand that everyone is playing the game and that each person has a big celebration awaiting the dog's success at locating him or her. Once the dog learns to love the game, simply calling out "Where are you?" will bring him running from wherever he is when he hears that all-important question.

The come command is recognized as one of the most important things to teach a dog, but there are trainers who work with thousands of dogs and never teach the actual word "come." Yet these

TEACHING HEEL

Heeling means that the dog walks beside the owner without pulling. It takes time and patience on the owner's part to succeed at teaching the dog that he (the owner) will not proceed unless the dog is walking calmly beside him. Neither pulling out ahead on the

"COME" ... BACK

Never call your dog to come to you for a correction or scold him when he reaches you. That is the quickest way to turn a come command into "Go away fast!" Dogs think only in the present tense, and your dog will connect the scolding with coming to you, not with the misbehavior of a few moments earlier.

leash nor lagging behind is acceptable.

Begin by holding the leash in your left hand as the dog sits beside your left leg. Move the loop end of the leash to your right hand, but keep your left hand short on the leash so that it keeps the dog in close next to you.

Say "Heel" and step forward on your left foot. Keep the dog close to you and take three steps. Stop and have the dog sit next to you in what we now call the heel position. Praise verbally, but do not touch the dog. Hesitate a moment and begin again with "Heel," taking three steps and stopping, at which point the dog is told to sit again.

Your goal here is to have the dog walk those three steps without pulling on the leash. Once he will walk calmly beside you for three steps without pulling, increase the number of steps you take to five. When he will walk politely beside you while you take five steps, you can increase the length of your walk to ten steps. Keep increasing the length of your stroll until the dog will walk quietly beside you without pulling as long as you want him to heel. When you stop heeling, indicate to the dog that the exercise is over by verbally praising as you pet him and say "OK, good dog." The "OK" is used as a release word, meaning that the exercise is finished and the dog is free to relax.

If you are dealing with a dog who insists on pulling you around, simply "put on your brakes" and stand your ground until the dog realizes that the two of you are not going anywhere until he is beside you and moving at your pace, not his. It may take some time just standing there to convince the dog that you are the leader and that you will be the one to decide on the direction and speed of your travel.

Each time the dog looks up at you or slows down to give a slack leash between the two of you, quietly praise him and say "Good

HEELING WELL
Teach your dog to heel in an enclosed area. Once you think the dog will obey reliably and you want to attempt advanced obedience exercises such as off-leash heeling, test him in a fenced-in area so he cannot run away.

heel. Good dog." Eventually, the dog will begin to respond and within a few days he will be walking politely beside you without pulling on the leash. At first, the training sessions should be kept short and very positive; soon the dog will be able to walk nicely with you for increasingly longer distances. Remember also to give the dog free time and the opportunity to run and play when you have finished heel practice.

WEANING OFF FOOD IN TRAINING

Food is used in training new behaviors. Once the dog understands what behavior goes with a specific command, it is time to

> **FETCH!**
> Play fetching games with your puppy in an enclosed area where he can retrieve his toy and bring it back to you. Always use a toy or object designated just for this purpose. Never use a shoe, sock or other item he may later confuse with those in your closet or underneath your chair.

start weaning him off the food treats. At first, give a treat after each exercise. Then, start to give a treat only after every other exercise. Mix up the times when you offer a food reward and the times when you only offer praise so that the dog will never know when he is going to receive both food and praise and when he is going to receive only praise. This is called a variable ratio reward system. It proves successful because there is always the chance that the owner will produce a treat, so the dog never stops trying for that reward. No matter what, *always* give verbal praise.

OBEDIENCE CLASSES

It is a good idea to enroll in an obedience class if one is available in your area. If yours is a show dog, handling classes would be more appropriate. Many areas have dog clubs that offer basic obedience training as

When engaging your Tosa in a game of fetch, be certain to select "Tosa-worthy" toys. This basketball was inflated a few tosses ago, but didn't stand a chance against the Tosa's jaws and teeth!

well as preparatory classes for obedience competition. There are also local dog trainers who offer similar classes.

At obedience trials, dogs can earn titles at various levels of competition. The beginning levels of obedience competition include basic behaviors such as sit, down, heel, etc. The more advanced levels of competition include jumping, retrieving, scent discrimination and signal work. The advanced levels require a dog and owner to put a lot of time and effort into their training. The titles that can be earned at these levels of competition are very prestigious.

OTHER ACTIVITIES FOR LIFE

Tosas are classified as working dogs, and they thrive on activities that require both mental and physical concentration. Tosas have been very successful in the show ring. Several dogs have been certified as therapy dogs and visit hospitals, convalescent homes and schools regularly. Another event in which Tosas excel is weight pulling. This makes maximum use of the drive and the strength of the Tosa breed. Several Tosas have excelled in agility, obedience and ring sports, and some have been trained as Schutzhund dogs.

However, don't limit activities with your Tosa to these public events. Your Tosa wants to

"work," even if this work is going for walks, practicing training exercises or wrestling with other dogs. Just keep your Tosa involved in your life; being part of your daily routine stimulates him. Take your Tosa on daily errands or on

HOW TO WEAN THE "TREAT HOG"

If you have trained your dog by rewarding him with a treat each time he performs a command, he may soon decide that without the treat, he won't sit, stay or come. The best way to fix this problem is to start asking your dog to do certain commands twice before being rewarded. Slowly increase the number of commands given and then vary the number: three sits and a treat one day, five sits for a biscuit the next day, etc. Your dog will soon realize that there is no set number of sits before he gets his reward and he'll likely do it the first time you ask in the hope of being rewarded sooner rather than later.

East West Seishen, undergoing protection training. Since the Tosa's natural protective instincts are strong, some breeders do not encourage Schutzhund work for the Tosa. Only approach attack training with the assistance of a qualified professional.

COMPETING WITH YOUR TOSA

Tosas excel in competitions. Keep them engaged and enthusiastic. Agility and working trials have been great venues for Tosas because these activities highlight both their superior athletic abilities and their high motivation to please. Start your Tosa's training for these activities at an appropriate early age (after 12 months old for agility).

TOSAS IN SCHUTZHUND

As a Japanese Tosa owner, you have the opportunity to participate in Schutzhund competition if you choose. Schutzhund originated in Germany as a test to determine the best quality dogs to be used for breeding stock. Breeders continue to use it as a way to evaluate working ability and temperament. There are three levels in Schutzhund trials: SchH. I, SchH. II and SchH. III, with each level being progressively more difficult to complete successfully. Each level consists of training, obedience and protection phases. Training for Schutzhund is intense and must be practiced consistently to keep the dog keen. The experience of Schutzhund training is very rewarding for dog and owner, although caution must be taken with such a naturally protective breed.

your walk to the mailbox. He will appreciate any activity that you do with him. Tosas are excellent traveling companions; we have taken Tosas all over the world and they are fantastic hotel mates, clean and courteous.

One of the most pleasurable and rewarding activities for you and your Tosa could be training. Tosas thrive when they are mentally and physically challenged and stimulated. It is assumed that you will teach your Tosa the basic commands—sit, stay, down, come, out, etc.—and we know that putting your Tosa through these basic steps on a regular basis strengthens the bond between you. But this is just a starting point for training your Tosa. The breed is very intelligent and picks up commands easily.

Look for things that your Tosa has a natural tendency towards and turn them into a game. One Tosa owner observed that his dog was very interested in the swimming pool. He encouraged

her to try the water and she soon was swimming laps with great gusto. One of our Tosas liked to put his paws on a person's lap, then on the person's shoulders. We taught him only to do this at our command and it became a great party trick. As you get to know your Tosa and his individual personality traits, his aptitudes and what he enjoys, you can develop these things further through your training and use them to make training enjoyable for all involved.

Like a Tosa to water...? You may be surprised at what your Tosa enjoys and what he's good at; take advantage of these things to develop his abilities and keep him motivated to learn more.

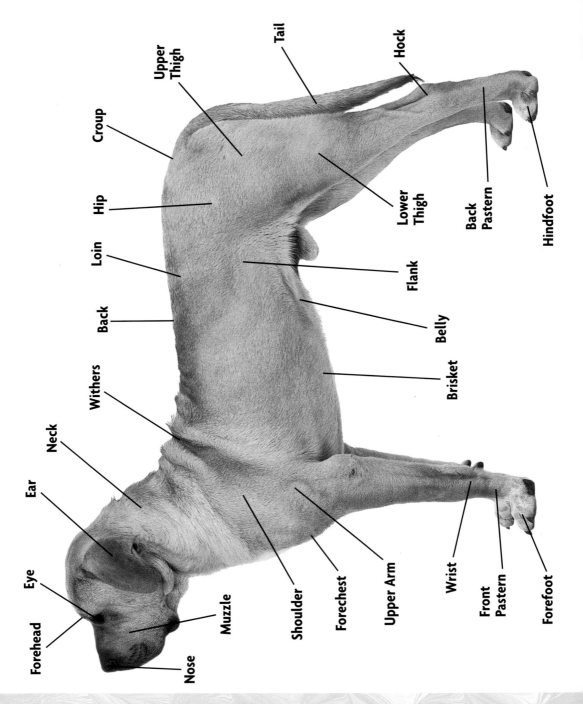

PHYSICAL STRUCTURE OF THE JAPANESE TOSA

JAPANESE TOSA

Dogs suffer from many of the same physical illnesses as people. Since people usually know more about human diseases than canine maladies, many of the terms used in this chapter will be familiar but not necessarily those used by veterinarians. For example, we will use the familiar term *x-ray* instead of *radiograph*. We will also use the familiar term *symptoms*, even though dogs don't have symptoms, which are verbal descriptions of something the patient feels or observes himself that he regards as abnormal. Dogs have *clinical signs* since they cannot speak, so we have to look for these clinical signs…but we still use the term *symptoms* in the book.

Medicine is a constantly changing art, with of course scientific input as well. Things alter as we learn more and more about basic sciences such as genetics and biochemistry, and have use of more sophisticated imaging techniques like Computer Aided Tomography (CAT scans) or Magnetic Resonance Imaging (MRI scans). There is academic dispute about many canine maladies, so different vets treat them in different ways. For example, some vets place greater emphasis on surgical techniques than others.

SELECTING A QUALIFIED VET
Your selection of a vet should be based on personal recommendation for his skills with pet animals, especially dogs, and, if possible, especially giant breeds like the Tosa. If the vet is based nearby, it will be helpful because you might have an emergency or need to make multiple visits for treatments.

All vets are licensed and should be capable of dealing with routine medical issues such as infections, injuries and the promotion of health (for example, by vaccination). If the problem affecting your dog is more complex, your vet will refer your pet to someone with a more detailed knowledge of what is wrong. This will usually be a specialist at the nearest university veterinary school who concentrates in the field relevant to your dog's problem (e.g., veterinary dermatology, ophthalmology, oncology, etc.).

Veterinary procedures are very costly and, as the treatments available improve, they are going to become more expensive. It is

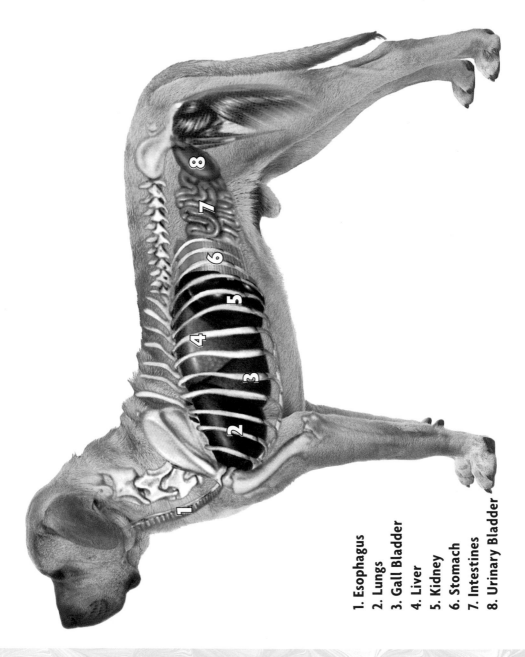

1. Esophagus
2. Lungs
3. Gall Bladder
4. Liver
5. Kidney
6. Stomach
7. Intestines
8. Urinary Bladder

INTERNAL ORGANS OF THE JAPANESE TOSA

quite acceptable to discuss matters of cost with your vet; if there is more than one treatment option, cost may be a factor in deciding which route to take.

Veterinary insurance is becoming more readily available for dog owners. While some policies cover emergencies only, more extensive (and more expensive) policies will include routine care like checkups and vaccinations.

PREVENTATIVE MEDICINE

It is much easier, less costly and more effective to practice preventative medicine than to fight bouts of illness and disease. Properly bred puppies of all breeds come from parents that were selected based upon their genetic-disease profiles. The puppies' mother should have been vaccinated, free of all internal and external parasites and properly nourished. For these reasons, a visit to the vet who cared for the dam is recommended if at all possible. The dam passes disease resistance to her puppies, which should last from eight to ten weeks. Unfortunately, she can also pass on parasites and infection. This is why knowledge about her health is useful in learning more about the health of the puppies.

WEANING TO FIVE MONTHS OLD

Puppies should be weaned by the time they are two months old. A puppy that remains for at least

Breakdown of Veterinary Income by Category

%	Category
2%	Dentistry
4%	Radiology
12%	Surgery
15%	Vaccinations
19%	Laboratory
23%	Examinations
25%	Medicines

A typical vet's income, categorized according to services performed. This survey dealt with small-animal (pets) practices.

eight weeks with his dam and littermates usually adapts better to other dogs and people later in his life.

Sometimes new owners have their puppy examined by a vet immediately, which is a good idea unless the puppy is overtired by a long journey. In that case the pup should visit the vet within the next day or two.

The puppy will have his teeth examined and his skeletal conformation and general health checked prior to certification by the vet. Puppies in certain breeds have problems with their kneecaps, cataracts and other eye problems, heart murmurs and undescended testicles. Your vet might have training in temperament evaluation. He will certainly set up your pup's vaccination schedule at the first visit.

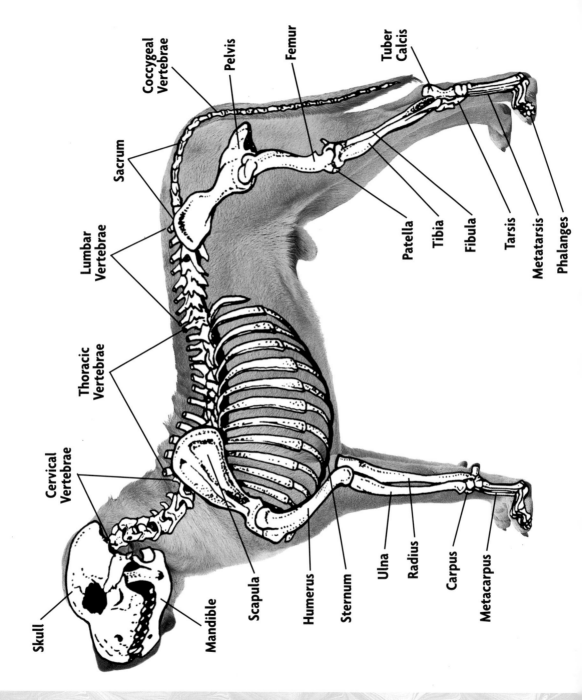

Coccygeal Vertebrae

Pelvis

Femur

Tuber Calcis

Sacrum

Lumbar Vertebrae

Thoracic Vertebrae

Cervical Vertebrae

Patella

Tibia

Fibula

Tarsis

Metatarsis

Phalanges

Skull

Mandible

Scapula

Humerus

Sternum

Ulna

Radius

Carpus

Metacarpus

SKELETAL STRUCTURE OF THE JAPANESE TOSA

Vaccination Scheduling

Most vaccinations are given by injection and should only be given by a vet. Both he and you should keep a record of the date of the injection, the identification of the vaccine and the amount given. Some vets give a first vaccination at eight weeks, but most dog breeders prefer the course not to commence until about ten weeks because of the risk of interaction with the antibodies produced by the mother. The vaccination scheduling is usually based on a 15-day cycle. You must take your vet's advice as to when to vaccinate, as this may differ according to the vaccine used.

The usual vaccines contain immunizing doses of several different viruses such as distemper, parvovirus, parainfluenza and hepatitis. There are other vaccines available when the puppy is at risk. You should rely upon professional advice. This is especially true for the booster immunizations. Most vaccination programs require a booster when the puppy is a year old and once a year thereafter. In some cases, circumstances may require more or less frequent immunizations.

DISEASE REFERENCE CHART

	What is it?	What causes it?	Symptoms
Leptospirosis	Severe disease that affects the internal organs; can be spread to people.	A bacterium, which is often carried by rodents, that enters through mucous membranes and spreads quickly throughout the body.	Range from fever, vomiting and loss of appetite in less severe cases to shock, irreversible kidney damage and possibly death in most severe cases.
Rabies	Potentially deadly virus that infects warm-blooded mammals.	Bite from a carrier of the virus, mainly wild animals.	1st stage: dog exhibits change in behavior, fear. 2nd stage: dog's behavior becomes more aggressive. 3rd stage: loss of coordination, trouble with bodily functions.
Parvovirus	Highly contagious virus, potentially deadly.	Ingestion of the virus, which is usually spread through the feces of infected dogs.	Most common: severe diarrhea. Also vomiting, fatigue, lack of appetite.
Canine cough	Contagious respiratory infection.	Combination of types of bacteria and virus. Most common: *Bordetella bronchiseptica* bacteria and parainfluenza virus.	Chronic cough.
Distemper	Disease primarily affecting respiratory and nervous system.	Virus that is related to the human measles virus.	Mild symptoms such as fever, lack of appetite and mucus secretion progress to evidence of brain damage, "hard pad."
Hepatitis	Virus primarily affecting the liver.	Canine adenovirus type I (CAV-1). Enters system when dog breathes in particles.	Lesser symptoms include listlessness, diarrhea, vomiting. More severe symptoms include "blue-eye" (clumps of virus in eye).
Coronavirus	Virus resulting in digestive problems.	Virus is spread through infected dog's feces.	Stomach upset evidenced by lack of appetite, vomiting, diarrhea.

First Aid at a Glance

Burns
Place the affected area under cool water; use ice if only a small area is burnt.

Bee stings/Insect bites
Apply ice to relieve swelling; antihistamine dosed properly.

Animal bites
Clean any bleeding area; apply pressure until bleeding subsides; go to the vet.

Spider bites
Use cold compress and a pressurized pack to inhibit venom's spreading.

Antifreeze poisoning
Induce vomiting with hydrogen peroxide. Seek *immediate* veterinary help!

Fish hooks
Removal best handled by vet; hook must be cut in order to remove.

Snake bites
Pack ice around bite; contact vet quickly; identify snake for proper antivenin.

Car accident
Move dog from roadway with blanket; seek veterinary aid.

Shock
Calm the dog; keep him warm; seek immediate veterinary help.

Nosebleed
Apply cold compress to the nose; apply pressure to any visible abrasion.

Bleeding
Apply pressure above the area; treat wound by applying a cotton pack.

Heat stroke
Submerge dog in cold bath; cool down with fresh air and water; go to the vet.

Frostbite/Hypothermia
Warm the dog with a warm bath, electric blankets or hot water bottles.

Abrasions
Clean the wound and wash out thoroughly with fresh water; apply antiseptic.

 Remember: an injured dog may attempt to bite a helping hand from fear and confusion. Always muzzle the dog before trying to offer assistance.

Canine cough, more formally known as tracheobronchitis, is immunized against with a vaccine that is sprayed into the dog's nostrils. Canine cough is usually included in routine vaccination, but it is often not as effective as the vaccines for other major diseases.

FIVE MONTHS TO ONE YEAR OF AGE

Unless you intend to breed or show your dog, neutering the puppy at an appropriate age is recommended. Discuss this with your vet, as opinions vary regarding the best age at which to have this done. Neutering/spaying has proven to be extremely beneficial to male and female dogs, respectively. Besides eliminating the possibility of pregnancy, it inhibits (but does not prevent) breast cancer in bitches and prostate cancer in male dogs.

Your vet should provide your puppy with a thorough dental evaluation at six months of age, ascertaining whether all of the permanent teeth have erupted properly. A home dental-care regimen should be initiated at six months, including brushing weekly and providing good

HEALTH AND VACCINATION SCHEDULE

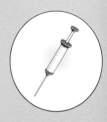

AGE IN WEEKS:	6TH	8TH	10TH	12TH	14TH	16TH	20-24TH	52ND
Worm Control	✔	✔	✔	✔	✔	✔	✔	
Neutering								✔
Heartworm		✔		✔		✔	✔	
Parvovirus	✔		✔		✔		✔	✔
Distemper		✔		✔		✔		✔
Hepatitis		✔		✔		✔		✔
Leptospirosis								✔
Parainfluenza	✔		✔		✔			✔
Dental Examination		✔					✔	✔
Complete Physical		✔					✔	✔
Coronavirus				✔			✔	✔
Canine Cough	✔							
Hip Dysplasia								✔
Rabies							✔	

Vaccinations are not instantly effective. It takes about two weeks for the dog's immune system to develop antibodies. Most vaccinations require annual booster shots. Your vet should guide you in this regard.

dental devices (such as nylon bones). Regular dental care promotes healthy teeth, fresh breath and a longer life.

DOGS OLDER THAN ONE YEAR

Continue to visit the vet at least once a year. There is no such disease as "old age," but bodily functions do change with age. The eyes and ears are no longer as efficient. Liver, kidney and intestinal functions often decline. Proper dietary changes, recommended by your vet, can make life more pleasant for your aging Tosa and you.

SKIN PROBLEMS

Vets are consulted by dog owners for skin problems more than for any other group of diseases or maladies. A dog's skin is as sensitive, if not more so, than human skin, and both suffer from almost the same ailments (though the occurrence of acne in dogs is rare!). For this reason, veterinary dermatology has developed into a specialty practiced by many vets.

Since many skin problems have visual symptoms that are almost identical, it requires the skill of an experienced veterinary dermatologist to identify and cure many of the more severe skin disorders. Pet shops sell many treatments for skin problems, but most of the treatments are directed at symptoms and not at the underlying problem(s). If your dog is suffering from a skin disorder, you should seek professional assistance as quickly as possible. As with all diseases, the earlier a problem is identified and treated, the more likely it is that the cure will be successful.

HEREDITARY SKIN DISORDERS

Veterinary dermatologists are currently researching a number of skin disorders that are believed to have hereditary bases. These inherited diseases are transmitted by both parents, who appear (phenotypically) normal but have a recessive gene for the disease, meaning that they carry, but are not affected by, the disease. These diseases pose serious problems to breeders because in some instances there are no methods of identifying carriers. Often the secondary diseases associated with these skin conditions are even more debilitating than the skin disorders themselves, including cancers and respiratory problems.

Among the hereditary skin disorders for which the mode of inheritance is known are acrodermatitis, cutaneous asthenia (Ehlers-Danlos syndrome), sebaceous adenitis, cyclic hematopoiesis, dermatomyositis, IgA deficiency, color dilution alopecia and nodular dermatofibrosis. Some of these disorders are limited to one or two breeds, while others affect a large number of breeds. All inherited diseases must be diagnosed and treated by a veterinary specialist.

PARASITE BITES

Many of us are allergic to insect bites. The bites itch, erupt and may even become infected. Dogs have the same reaction to fleas, ticks and/or mites. When an insect lands on you, you have the chance to whisk it away with your hand. Unfortunately, when a dog is bitten by a flea, tick or mite, he can only scratch it away or bite it. By the time the dog has been bitten, the parasite has done some of its damage. It may also have laid eggs, which will cause further problems in the near future. The itching from parasite bites is probably due to the saliva injected into the site when the parasite sucks the dog's blood.

AIRBORNE ALLERGIES

An interesting allergy is pollen allergy. Humans have hay fever with which they suffer from during the pollinating season. Many dogs suffer from the same allergies. When the pollen count is high, your dog might suffer, but don't expect him to sneeze and have a runny nose like a human would. Dogs react to pollen allergies in the same way that they react to fleas—they scratch and bite themselves.

Dogs, like humans, can be tested for allergens. Discuss the testing with your vet.

ACRAL LICK GRANULOMA

Many large dogs have a very poorly understood syndrome called acral lick granuloma. The manifestation of the problem is the dog's tireless attack at a specific area of the body, almost always the legs or paws. The dog licks so intensively that he removes the hair and skin, leaving an ugly, large wound. Tiny protuberances, which are outgrowths of new capillaries, bead on the surface of the wound. Owners who notice their dogs' biting and

Grass allergies are nothing to sneeze at! Many dogs have reaction to airborne allergens in early spring and late summer.

chewing at their extremities should have the vet determine the cause. If lick granuloma is identified, although there is no absolute cure, corticosteroids are one common treatment.

FOOD PROBLEMS

FOOD ALLERGIES
Dogs are allergic to many foods that are best-sellers and highly recommended by breeders and vets. Changing the brand of food that you buy may not eliminate the problem if the element to which the dog is allergic is contained in the new brand.

Recognizing a food allergy can be difficult. Humans often have rashes when they eat foods to which they are allergic, or have swelling of the lips or eyes. Dogs do not usually develop rashes, but react in the same way as they to an airborne or bite allergy— they itch, scratch and bite. While pollen allergies and parasite bites are usually seasonal, pollen allergies are year-round problems.

TREATING FOOD ALLERGY
Diagnosis of food allergy is based on a two- to four-week dietary trial with a home-cooked diet fed to the exclusion of all other foods. The diet should consist of boiled rice or potato with a source of protein that the dog has never eaten before, such as fresh or frozen fish, lamb or even something as exotic as pheasant. Water has to be the only drink, and it is really important that no other foods are fed during this trial. If the dog's condition improves, you will need to try the original diet once again to see if the itching resumes. If it does, then this confirms the diagnosis that the dog is allergic to his original diet. The treatment is long-term feeding of something that does not distress the dog's skin, which may be in the form of one of the commercially available hypoallergenic diets or the home-made diet that you created for the allergy trial.

FOOD INTOLERANCE
Food intolerance is the inability of the dog to completely digest certain foods. This occurs because the dog does not have the chemicals necessary to digest some foodstuffs. These chemicals are called enzymes. All puppies have the enzymes necessary to digest canine milk, but some dogs do not have the enzymes to digest a very different form of milk that is commonly found in human households—milk from cows. In such dogs, drinking cows' milk results in loose bowels, stomach pains and the passage of gas.

Dogs often do not have the enzymes to digest soy or other beans. The treatment is to exclude the foodstuffs that upset your Tosa's digestion.

Number-One Killer Disease in Dogs: CANCER

In every age, there is a word associated with a disease or plague that causes humans to shudder. In the 21st century, that word is "cancer." Just as cancer is the leading cause of death in humans, it claims nearly half the lives of dogs that die from a natural disease as well as half the dogs that die over the age of ten years.

Described as a genetic disease, cancer becomes a greater risk as the dog ages. Veterinarians and dog owners have become increasingly aware of the threat of cancer to dogs. Statistics reveal that one dog in every five will develop cancer, the most common of which is skin cancer. Many cancers, including prostate, ovarian and breast cancer, can be avoided by spaying and neutering our dogs by the age of six months.

Early detection of cancer can save or extend your dog's life, so it is absolutely vital for owners to have their dogs examined by a qualified vet or oncologist immediately upon detection of any abnormality. Certain dietary guidelines have also proven to reduce the onset and spread of cancer. Foods based on fish rather than beef, due to the presence of Omega-3 fatty acids, are recommended. Other amino acids such as glutamine have significant benefits for canines, particularly those breeds that show a greater susceptibility to cancer.

Cancer management and treatments promise hope for future generations of canines. Since the disease is genetic, breeders should never breed a dog whose parents, grandparents and any related siblings have developed cancer. It is difficult to know whether to exclude an otherwise healthy dog from a breeding program as the disease does not manifest itself until the dog's senior years.

RECOGNIZE CANCER WARNING SIGNS

Since early detection can possibly rescue your dog from becoming a cancer statistic, it is essential for owners to recognize the possible signs and seek the assistance of a qualified professional.

- Abnormal bumps or lumps that continue to grow
- Bleeding or discharge from any body cavity
- Persistent stiffness or lameness
- Recurrent sores or sores that do not heal
- Inappetence
- Breathing difficulties
- Weight loss
- Bad breath or odors
- General malaise and fatigue
- Eating and swallowing problems
- Difficulty urinating and defecating

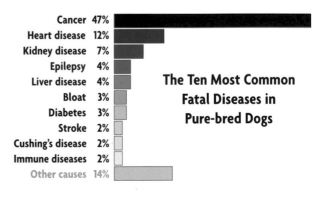

Disease	%
Cancer	47%
Heart disease	12%
Kidney disease	7%
Epilepsy	4%
Liver disease	4%
Bloat	3%
Diabetes	3%
Stroke	2%
Cushing's disease	2%
Immune diseases	2%
Other causes	14%

The Ten Most Common Fatal Diseases in Pure-bred Dogs

A male dog flea, *Ctenocephalides canis.*

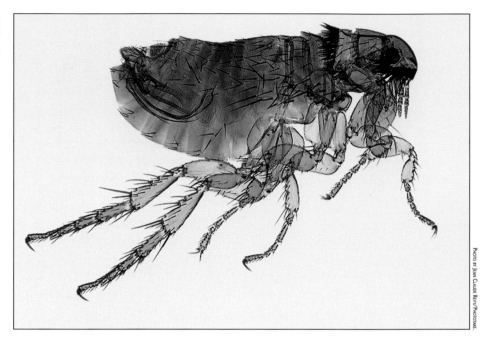

PHOTO BY JEAN CLAUDE REVY/PHOTOTAKE.

EXTERNAL PARASITES

FLEAS

Of all the problems to which dogs are prone, none is more well known and frustrating than fleas. Flea infestation is relatively simple to cure but difficult to prevent. Parasites that are harbored inside the body are a bit more difficult to eradicate but they are easier to control.

To control flea infestation, you have to understand the flea's life cycle. Fleas are often thought of as a summertime problem, but centrally heated homes have changed the patterns and fleas can be found at any time of the year. The most effective method of flea control is a two-stage approach: one stage to kill the adult fleas, and the other to control the development of pre-adult fleas. Unfortunately, no single active ingredient is effective against all stages of the life cycle.

FLEA KILLER CAUTION— "POISON"

Flea-killers are poisonous. You should not spray these toxic chemicals on areas of a dog's body that he licks, including his genitals and his face. Flea killers taken internally are a better answer, but check with your vet in case internal therapy is not advised for your dog.

LIFE CYCLE STAGES

During its life, a flea will pass through four life stages: egg, larva, pupa or nymph and adult. The adult stage is the most visible and irritating stage of the flea life cycle, and this is why the majority of flea-control products concentrate on this stage. The fact is that adult fleas account for only 1% of the total flea population, and the other 99% exist in pre-adult stages, i.e., eggs, larvae and nymphs. The pre-adult stages are barely visible to the naked eye.

THE LIFE CYCLE OF THE FLEA

Eggs are laid on the dog, usually in quantities of about 20 or 30, several times a day. The adult female flea must have a blood meal before each egg-laying session. When first laid, the eggs will cling to the dog's hair, as the eggs are still moist. However, they will quickly dry out and fall from the dog, especially if the dog moves around or scratches. Many eggs will fall off in the dog's favorite area or an area in which he spends a lot of time, such as his bed.

Once the eggs fall from the dog onto the carpet or furniture, they will hatch into larvae. This takes from one to ten days. Larvae are not particularly mobile and will usually travel only a few inches from where they hatch. However, they do have a tendency to move away from bright light and heavy

> ***EN GARDE:***
> **CATCHING FLEAS OFF GUARD!**
> Consider the following ways to arm yourself against fleas:
> - Add a small amount of pennyroyal or eucalyptus oil to your dog's bath. These natural remedies repel fleas.
> - Supplement your dog's food with fresh garlic (minced or grated) and a hearty amount of brewer's yeast, both of which ward off fleas.
> - Use a flea comb on your dog daily. Submerge fleas in a cup of bleach to kill them quickly.
> - Confine the dog to only a few rooms to limit the spread of fleas in the home.
> - Vacuum daily...and get all of the crevices! Dispose of the bag every few days until the problem is under control.
> - Wash your dog's bedding daily. Cover cushions where your dog sleeps with towels, and wash the towels often.

traffic—under furniture and behind doors are common places to find high quantities of flea larvae.

The flea larvae feed on dead organic matter, including adult flea feces, until they are ready to change into adult fleas. Fleas will usually remain as larvae for around seven days. After this period, the larvae will pupate into protective pupae. While inside the pupae, the larvae will undergo metamorphosis and change into adult fleas. This can take as little time as a few days, but the adult fleas can remain inside the pupae waiting to hatch for up to two years. The pupae are signaled to hatch by certain stimuli, such as physical pressure—the pupae's being stepped on, heat from an animal's lying on the pupae or increased carbon-dioxide levels and vibrations—indicating that a suitable host is available.

Once hatched, the adult flea must feed within a few days. Once the adult flea finds a host, it will not leave voluntarily. It only becomes dislodged by grooming or the host animal's scratching. The adult flea will remain on the

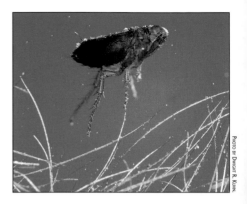

PHOTO BY DWIGHT R. KUHN

host for the duration of its life unless forcibly removed.

TREATING THE ENVIRONMENT AND THE DOG

Treating fleas should be a two-pronged attack. First, the environment needs to be treated; this includes carpets and furniture, especially the dog's bedding and areas underneath furniture. The environment should be treated with a household spray containing an Insect Growth Regulator (IGR) and an insecticide to kill the adult fleas. Most IGRs are effective against eggs and larvae; they actually mimic the fleas' own hormones and stop the eggs and larvae from developing into adult fleas. There are currently no treatments available to attack the pupa stage of the life cycle, so the adult insecticide is used to kill the newly hatched adult fleas before they find a host. Most IGRs are active for many months, while adult insecticides are only active

A scanning electron micrograph of a dog or cat flea, *Ctenocephalides,* magnified more than 100x. This image has been colorized for effect.

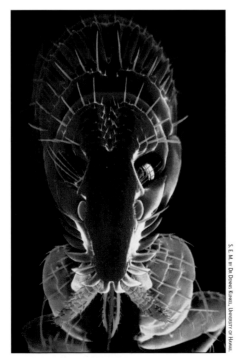

S. E. M. BY DR. DENNIS KUNKEL, UNIVERSITY OF HAWAII

THE LIFE CYCLE OF THE FLEA

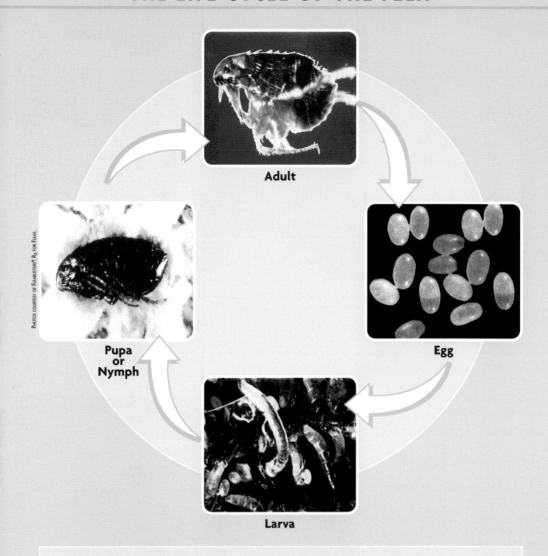

Adult

Egg

Larva

Pupa
or
Nymph

Fleas have been around for millions of years and have adapted to changing host animals. They are able to go through a complete life cycle in less than one month or they can extend their lives to almost two years by remaining as pupae or cocoons. They do not need blood or any other food for up to 20 months.

INSECT GROWTH REGULATOR (IGR)

Two types of products should be used when treating fleas—a product to treat the pet and a product to treat the home. Adult fleas represent less than 1% of the flea population. The pre-adult fleas (eggs, larvae and pupae) represent more than 99% of the flea population and are found in the environment; it is in the case of pre-adult fleas that products containing an Insect Growth Regulator (IGR) should be used in the home.

IGRs are a new class of compounds used to prevent the development of insects. They do not kill the insect outright, but instead use the insect's biology against it to stop it from completing its growth. Products that contain methoprene are the world's first and leading IGRs. Used to control fleas and other insects, this type of IGR will stop flea larvae from developing and protect the house for up to seven months.

The American dog tick, Dermacentor variabilis, is probably the most common tick found on dogs. Look at the strength in its eight legs! No wonder it's hard to detach them.

for a few days.

When treating with a household spray, it is a good idea to vacuum before applying the product. This stimulates as many pupae as possible to hatch into adult fleas. The vacuum cleaner should also be treated with an insecticide to prevent the eggs and larvae that have been collected in the vacuum bag from hatching.

The second stage of treatment is to apply an adult insecticide to the dog. Traditionally, this would be in the form of a collar or a spray, but more recent innovations include digestible insecticides that poison the fleas when they ingest the dog's blood. Alternatively, there are drops that, when placed on the back of the dog's neck, spread throughout the hair and skin to kill adult fleas.

TICKS

Though not as common as fleas, ticks are found all over the tropical and temperate world. They don't bite, like fleas; they harpoon. They dig their sharp proboscis (nose) into the dog's skin and drink the blood. Their only food and drink is dog's

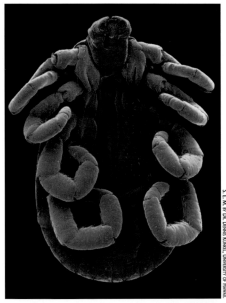

S. E. M. BY DR. DENNIS KUNKEL, UNIVERSITY OF HAWAII.

blood. Dogs can get Lyme disease, Rocky Mountain spotted fever, tick bite paralysis and many other diseases from ticks. They may live where fleas are found and they like to hide in cracks or seams in walls. They are controlled the same way fleas are controlled.

The American dog tick, *Dermacentor variabilis*, may well be the most common dog tick in many geographical areas, especially those areas where the climate is hot and humid. Most dog ticks have life expectancies of a week to six months, depending upon climatic conditions. They can neither jump nor fly, but they can crawl slowly and can range up to 16 feet to reach a sleeping or unsuspecting dog.

MITES

Just as fleas and ticks can be problematic for your dog, mites can also lead to an itchy nuisance. Microscopic in size, mites are related to ticks and generally take up permanent residence on their host animal— in this case, your dog! The term *mange* refers to any infestation caused by one of the mighty mites, of which there are six varieties that concern dog owners.

Demodex mites cause a condition known as demodicosis (sometimes called red mange or

DEER-TICK CROSSING
The great outdoors may be fun for your dog, but it also is a home to dangerous ticks. Deer ticks carry a bacterium known as *Borrelia burgdorferi* and are most active in the autumn and spring. When infections are caught early, penicillin and tetracycline are effective antibiotics, but, if left untreated, the bacteria may cause neurological, kidney and cardiac problems as well as long-term trouble with walking and painful joints.

S. E. M. by Dr. Andrew Spielman/Phototake.

Photo by Dr. Dennis Kunkel, University of Hawaii.

The head of an American dog tick, *Dermacentor variabilis*, enlarged and colorized for effect.

The mange mite, *Psoroptes bovis*, can infest cattle and other domestic animals.

PHOTO BY JAMES HAYDEN/YOAV/PHOTOTAKE

follicular mange), in which the mites live in the dog's hair follicles and sebaceous glands in larger-than-normal numbers. This type of mange is commonly passed from the dam to her puppies and usually shows up on the puppies' muzzles, though demodicosis is not transferable from one normal dog to another. Most dogs recover from this type of mange without any treatment, though topical therapies are commonly prescribed by the vet.

Human lice look like dog lice; the two are closely related.

PHOTO BY DWIGHT R. KUHN.

The *Cheyletiellosis* mite is the hook-mouthed culprit associated with "walking dandruff," a condition that affects dogs as well as cats and rabbits. This mite lives on the surface of the animal's skin and is readily transferable through direct or indirect contact with an affected animal. The dandruff is present in the form of scaly skin, which may or may not be itchy. If not treated, this mange can affect a whole kennel of dogs and can be spread to humans as well.

The *Sarcoptes* mite causes intense itching on the dog in the form of a condition known as scabies or sarcoptic mange. The cycle of the *Sarcoptes* mite lasts about three weeks, and the mites live in the top layer of the dog's skin (epidermis), preferably in areas with little hair. Scabies is highly contagious and can be passed to humans. Sometimes an allergic reaction to the mite worsens the severe itching associated with sarcoptic mange.

Ear mites, *Otodectes cynotis,* lead to otodectic mange, which most commonly affects the outer ear canal of the dog, though other areas can be affected as well. Dogs with ear-mite infestation commonly scratch at their ears, causing further irritation, and shake their heads. Dark brown droppings in the outer ear confirm the diagnosis. Your vet can prescribe a treatment to flush out the ears and kill any eggs in the ears. A complete month of treatment is necessary to cure the mange.

Two other mites, less common in dogs, include *Dermanyssus gallinae* (the poultry or red mite) and *Eutrombicula alfreddugesi* (the North American mite associated with trombiculidiasis or chigger infestation). The poultry mite frequently lives on chickens, but can transfer to dogs who spend time near farm animals. Chigger infestation affects dogs in the

NOT A DROP TO DRINK
Never allow your dog to swim in polluted water or public areas where water quality can be suspect. Even perfectly clear water can harbor parasites, many of which can cause serious to fatal illnesses in canines. Areas inhabited by waterfowl and other wildlife are especially dangerous.

Central US who have exposure to woodlands. The types of mange caused by both of these mites are treatable by vets.

INTERNAL PARASITES
Most animals—fishes, birds and mammals, including dogs and humans—have worms and other parasites that live inside their bodies. According to Dr. Herbert R. Axelrod, the fish pathologist, there are two kinds of parasites: dumb and smart. The smart parasites live in peaceful cooperation with their hosts (symbiosis), while the dumb parasites kill their hosts. Most worm infections are relatively easy to control. If they are not controlled, they weaken the host dog to the point that other medical problems occur, but they do not kill the host as dumb parasites would.

A brown dog tick, *Rhipicephalus sanguineus,* is an uncommon but annoying tick found on dogs. Photo by Carolina Biological Supply/Phototake.

DO NOT MIX
Never mix parasite-control products without first consulting your vet. Some products can become toxic when combined with others and can cause fatal consequences.

Photo by Carolina Biological Supply/Phototake.

The roundworm *Rhabditis* can infect both dogs and humans.

The roundworm, *Ascaris lumbricoides.*

ROUNDWORMS

Average-size dogs can pass 1,360,000 roundworm eggs every day. For example, if there were only 1 million dogs in the world, the world would be saturated with thousands of tons of dog feces. These feces would contain around 15,000,000,000 roundworm eggs.

Up to 31% of home yards and children's sand boxes in the US contain roundworm eggs.

Flushing dog's feces down the toilet is not a safe practice because the usual sewage treatments do not destroy roundworm eggs.

Infected puppies start shedding roundworm eggs at three weeks of age. They can be infected by their mother's milk.

Roundworms

The roundworms that infect dogs are known scientifically as *Toxocara canis*. They live in the dog's intestines and shed eggs continually. It has been estimated that a dog produces about 6 or more ounces of feces every day. Each ounce of feces averages hundreds of thousands of roundworm eggs. There are no known areas in which dogs roam that do not contain roundworm eggs. The greatest danger of roundworms is that they infect people, too! It is wise to have your dog tested regularly for roundworms.

In young puppies, roundworms cause bloated bellies, diarrhea, coughing and vomiting, and are transmitted from the dam (through blood or milk). Affected puppies will not appear as animated as normal puppies. The worms appear spaghetti-like, measuring as long as 6 inches. Adult dogs can acquire roundworms through coprophagia (eating contaminated feces) or by killing rodents that carry roundworms.

Roundworm infection can kill puppies and cause severe problems in adults, as the hatched larvae travel to the lungs and trachea through the bloodstream. Cleanliness is the best preventative for roundworms. Always pick up after your dog and dispose of feces in appropriate receptacles.

Photo by Dwight R. Kuhn.

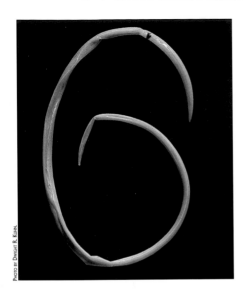

HOOKWORMS

In the United States, dog owners have to be concerned about four different species of hookworm, the most common and most serious of which is *Ancylostoma caninum,* which prefers warm climates. The others are *Ancylostoma braziliense, Ancylostoma tubaeforme* and *Uncinaria stenocephala,* the latter of which is a concern to dogs living in the Northern US and Canada, as this species prefers cold climates. Hookworms are dangerous to humans as well as to dogs and cats, and can be the cause of severe anemia due to iron deficiency. The worm uses its teeth to attach itself to the dog's intestines and changes the site of its attachment about six times per day. Each time the worm

repositions itself, the dog loses blood and can become anemic. *Ancylostoma caninum* is the most likely of the four species to cause anemia in the dog.

Symptoms of hookworm infection include dark stools, weight loss, general weakness, pale coloration and anemia, as well as possible skin problems. Fortunately, hookworms are easily purged from the affected dog with a number of medications that have proven effective. Discuss these with your vet. Most heartworm preventatives include a hookworm insecticide as well.

Owners also must be aware that hookworms can infect humans, who can acquire the larvae through exposure to contaminated feces. Since the worms cannot complete their life cycle on a human, the worms simply infest the skin and cause irritation. This condition is known as cutaneous larva migrans syndrome. As a preventative, use disposable gloves or a "poop-scoop" to pick up your dog's droppings and prevent your dog (or neighborhood cats) from defecating in children's play areas.

The hookworm, *Ancylostoma caninum.*

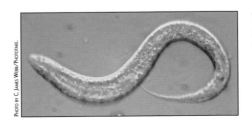

The infective stage of the hookworm larva.

TAPEWORMS

Humans, rats, squirrels, foxes, coyotes, wolves and domestic dogs are all susceptible to tapeworm infection. Except in humans, tapeworms are usually not a fatal infection. Infected individuals can harbor 1000 parasitic worms.

Tapeworms, like some other types of worm, are hermaphroditic, meaning male and female in the same worm.

If dogs eat infected rats or mice, or anything else infected with tapeworm, they get the tapeworm disease. One month after attaching to a dog's intestine, the worm starts shedding eggs. These eggs are infective immediately. Infective eggs can live for a few months without a host animal.

The head and rostellum (the round prominence on the scolex) of a tapeworm, which infects dogs and humans.

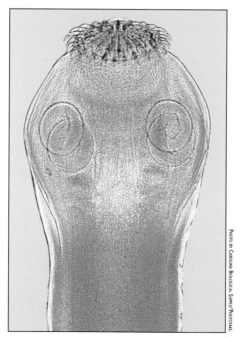

PHOTO BY CAROLINA BIOLOGICAL SUPPLY/PHOTOTAKE.

TAPEWORMS

There are many species of tapeworm, all of which are carried by fleas! The most common tapeworm affecting dogs is known as *Dipylidium caninum*. The dog eats the flea and starts the tapeworm cycle. Humans can also be infected with tapeworms—so don't eat fleas! Fleas are so small that your dog could pass them onto your hands, your plate or your food and thus make it possible for you to ingest a flea that is carrying tapeworm eggs.

While tapeworm infection is not life-threatening in dogs (smart parasite!), it can be the cause of a very serious liver disease for humans. About 50% of the humans infected with *Echinococcus multilocularis*, a type of tapeworm that causes alveolar hydatid, perish.

WHIPWORMS

In North America, whipworms are counted among the most common parasitic worms in dogs. The whipworm's scientific name is *Trichuris vulpis.* These worms attach themselves in the lower parts of the intestine, where they feed. Affected dogs may only experience upset tummies, colic and diarrhea. These worms, however, can live for months or years in the dog, beginning their larval stage in the small intestine, spending their adult stage in the large intestine and finally passing infective eggs through the dog's feces. The only way to detect whipworms is through a fecal examination, though this is not always foolproof. Treatment for whipworms is tricky, due to the worms' unusual life-cycle pattern, and very often dogs are reinfected due to exposure to infective eggs on the ground. The whipworm eggs can survive in the environment for as long as five years; thus, cleaning up droppings in your own backyard as well as in public places is absolutely essential for sanitation purposes and the health of your dog and others.

THREADWORMS

Though less common than round-worms, hookworms and those previously mentioned, thread-worms concern dog owners in the Southwestern US and Gulf Coast area where the climate is hot and humid. Living in the small intestine of the dog, this worm measures a mere 2 millimeters and is round in shape. Like that of the whipworm, the threadworm's life cycle is very complex and the eggs and larvae are passed through the feces. A deadly disease in humans, *Strongyloides* readily infects people, and the handling of feces is the most common means of transmission. Threadworms are most often seen in young puppies; bloody diarrhea and pneumonia are symptoms. Sick puppies must be isolated and treated immediately; vets recommend a follow-up treatment one month later.

HEARTWORM PREVENTATIVES

There are many heartworm preventatives on the market, many of which are sold at your veterinarian's office. These products can be given daily or monthly, depending on the manufacturer's instructions. All of these preventatives contain chemical insecticides directed at killing heartworms, which leads to some controversy among dog owners. In effect, heartworm preventatives are necessary evils, though you should determine how necessary based on your pet's lifestyle. There is no doubt that heartworm is a dreadful disease that threatens the lives of dogs. However, the likelihood of your dog's being bitten by an infected mosquito is slim in most places, and a mosquito-repellent (or an herbal remedy such as Wormwood or Black Walnut) is much safer for your dog and will not compromise his immune system (the way heartworm preventatives will). Should you decide to use the traditional preventative "medications," you can consider giving the pill every other or third month. Since the toxins in the pill will kill the heartworms at all stages of development, the pill would be effective in killing larvae, nymphs or adults, and it takes four months for the larvae to reach the adult stage. Thus, there is no rationale to poisoning the dog's system on a monthly basis. Lastly, do not give the pill during the winter months since there are no mosquitoes around to pass on their infection, unless you live in a tropical environment.

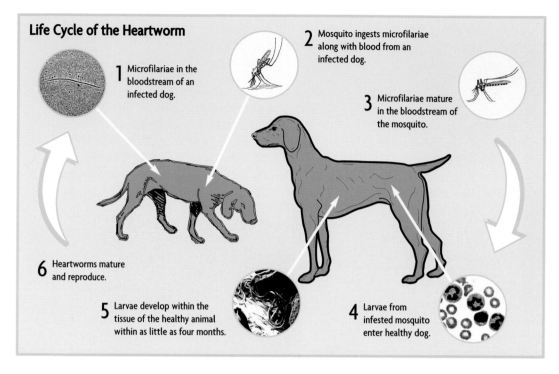

Life Cycle of the Heartworm

1 Microfilariae in the bloodstream of an infected dog.

2 Mosquito ingests microfilariae along with blood from an infected dog.

3 Microfilariae mature in the bloodstream of the mosquito.

6 Heartworms mature and reproduce.

5 Larvae develop within the tissue of the healthy animal within as little as four months.

4 Larvae from infested mosquito enter healthy dog.

HEARTWORMS

Heartworms are thin, extended worms up to 12 inches long, which live in a dog's heart and the major blood vessels surrounding it. Dogs may have up to 200 worms. Symptoms may be loss of energy, loss of appetite, coughing, the development of a pot belly and anemia.

Heartworms are transmitted by mosquitoes. The mosquito drinks the blood of an infected dog and takes in larvae with the blood. The larvae, called microfilariae, develop within the body of the mosquito and are passed on to the next dog bitten after the larvae mature. It takes two to three weeks for the larvae to develop to the infective stage within the body of the mosquito. Dogs are usually treated at about six weeks of age and maintained on a prophylactic dose given monthly.

Blood testing for heartworms is not necessarily indicative of how seriously your dog is infected. Although this is a dangerous disease, it is not easy for a dog to be infected. Discuss the various preventatives with your vet, as there are many different types now available. Together you can decide on a safe course of prevention for your dog.

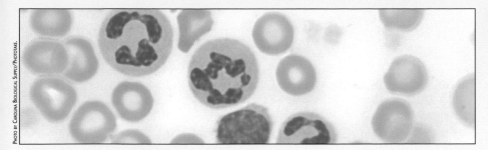

Magnified heartworm larvae, *Dirofilaria immitis.*

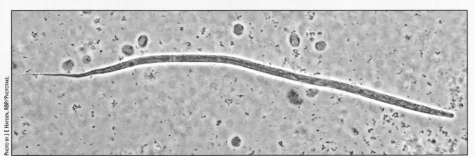

Heartworm, *Dirofilaria immitis.*

The heart of a dog infected with canine heartworm, *Dirofilaria immitis.*

HOMEOPATHY:
an alternative to conventional medicine

"Less is Most"

Using this principle, the strength of a homeopathic remedy is measured by the number of serial dilutions that were undertaken to create it. The greater the number of serial dilutions, the greater the strength of the homeopathic remedy. The potency of a remedy that has been made by making a dilution of 1 part in 100 parts (or 1/100) is 1c or 1cH. If this remedy is subjected to a series of further dilutions, each one being 1/100, a more dilute and stronger remedy is produced. If the remedy is diluted in this way six times, it is called 6c or 6cH. A dilution of 6c is 1 part in 1,000,000,000,000. In general, higher potencies in more frequent doses are better for acute symptoms and lower potencies in more infrequent doses are more useful for chronic, long-standing problems.

CURING OUR DOGS NATURALLY

Holistic medicine means treating the whole animal as a unique, perfect living being. Generally, holistic treatments do not suppress the symptoms that the body naturally produces, as do most medications prescribed by conventional doctors and vets. Holistic methods seek to cure disease by regaining balance and harmony in the patient's environment. Some of these methods include use of nutritional therapy, herbs, flower essences, aromatherapy, acupuncture, massage, chiropractic and, of course, the most popular holistic approach, homeopathy.

Homeopathy is a theory or system of treating illness with small doses of substances which, if administered in larger quantities, would produce the symptoms that the patient already has. This approach is often described as "like cures like." Although modern veterinary medicine is geared toward the "quick fix," homeopathy relies on the belief that, given the time, the body is able to heal itself and return to its natural, healthy state.

Choosing a remedy to cure a problem in our dogs is the difficult part of homeopathy. Consult with your vet for a professional diagnosis of your dog's symptoms. Often these symptoms require immediate conventional care. If your vet is willing and knowledgeable, you may attempt a homeopathic remedy. Be aware that cortisone prevents homeopathic remedies from working. There are hundreds of possibilities and combinations to cure many problems in dogs, from basic physical problems such as excessive shedding, fleas or other parasites, unattractive doggy odor, bad breath, upset tummy, obesity, dry, oily or dull coat, diarrhea, ear problems or eye discharge (including tears and dry or mucousy matter), to behavioral abnormalities such as fear of loud noises, habitual licking, poor appetite, excessive barking and various phobias. From alumina to zincum metallicum, the remedies span the planet and the imagination…from flowers and weeds to chemicals, insect droppings, diesel smoke and volcanic ash.

Using "Like to Treat Like"

Unlike conventional medicines that suppress symptoms, homeopathic remedies treat illnesses with small doses of substances that, if administered in larger quantities, would produce the symptoms that the patient already has. While the same homeopathic remedy can be used to treat different symptoms in different dogs, here are some interesting remedies and their uses.

Apis Mellifica
(made from honey bee venom) can be used for allergies or to reduce swelling that occurs in acutely infected kidneys.

Diesel Smoke
can be used to help control motion sickness.

Calcarea Fluorica
(made from calcium fluoride, which helps harden bone structure) can be useful in treating hard lumps in tissues.

Natrum Muriaticum
(made from common salt, sodium chloride) is useful in treating thin, thirsty dogs.

Nitricum Acidum
(made from nitric acid) is used for symptoms you would expect to see from contact with acids, such as lesions, especially where the skin joins the linings of body orifices or openings such as the lips and nostrils.

Symphytum
(made from the herb Knitbone, *Symphytum officianale*) is used to encourage bones to heal.

Urtica Urens
(made from the common stinging nettle) is used in treating painful, irritating rashes.

HOMEOPATHIC REMEDIES FOR YOUR DOG

Symptom/Ailment	Possible Remedy
ALLERGIES	Apis Mellifica 30c, Astacus Fluviatilis 6c, Pulsatilla 30c, Urtica Urens 6c
ALOPECIA	Alumina 30c, Lycopodium 30c, Sepia 30c, Thallium 6c
ANAL GLANDS (BLOCKED)	Hepar Sulphuris Calcareum 30c, Sanicula 6c, Silicea 6c
ARTHRITIS	Rhus Toxicodendron 6c, Bryonia Alba 6c
CANINE COUGH	Drosera 6c, Ipecacuanha 30c
CATARACT	Calcarea Carbonica 6c, Conium Maculatum 6c, Phosphorus 30c, Silicea 30c
CONSTIPATION	Alumina 6c, Carbo Vegetabilis 30c, Graphites 6c, Nitricum Acidum 30c, Silicea 6c
COUGHING	Aconitum Napellus 6c, Belladonna 30c, Hyoscyamus Niger 30c, Phosphorus 30c
DIARRHEA	Arsenicum Album 30c, Aconitum Napellus 6c, Chamomilla 30c, Mercurius Corrosivus 30c
DRY EYE	Zincum Metallicum 30c
EAR PROBLEMS	Aconitum Napellus 30c, Belladonna 30c, Hepar Sulphuris 30c, Tellurium 30c, Psorinum 200c
EYE PROBLEMS	Borax 6c, Aconitum Napellus 30c, Graphites 6c, Staphysagria 6c, Thuja Occidentalis 30c
GLAUCOMA	Aconitum Napellus 30c, Apis Mellifica 6c, Phosphorus 30c
HEAT STROKE	Belladonna 30c, Gelsemium Sempervirens 30c, Sulphur 30c
HICCOUGHS	Cinchona Deficinalis 6c
HIP DYSPLASIA	Colocynthis 6c, Rhus Toxicodendron 6c, Bryonia Alba 6c
INCONTINENCE	Argentum Nitricum 6c, Causticum 30c, Conium Maculatum 30c, Pulsatilla 30c, Sepia 30c
INSECT BITES	Apis Mellifica 30c, Cantharis 30c, Hypericum Perforatum 6c, Urtica Urens 30c
ITCHING	Alumina 30c, Arsenicum Album 30c, Carbo Vegetabilis 30c, Hypericum Perforatum 6c, Mezerium 6c, Sulphur 30c
MASTITIS	Apis Mellifica 30c, Belladonna 30c, Urtica Urens 1m
MOTION SICKNESS	Cocculus 6c, Petroleum 6c
PATELLAR LUXATION	Gelsemium Sempervirens 6c, Rhus Toxicodendron 6c
PENIS PROBLEMS	Aconitum Napellus 30c, Hepar Sulphuris Calcareum 30c, Pulsatilla 30c, Thuja Occidentalis 6c
PUPPY TEETHING	Calcarea Carbonica 6c, Chamomilla 6c, Phytolacca 6c

Recognizing a Sick Dog

Unlike colicky babies and cranky children, our canine charges cannot tell us when they are feeling ill. Therefore, there are a number of signs that owners can identify to know that their dogs are not feeling well.

Take note for physical manifestations such as:

- unusual, bad odor, including bad breath
- excessive shedding
- wax in the ears, chronic ear irritation
- oily, flaky, dull haircoat
- mucus, tearing or similar discharge in the eyes
- fleas or mites
- mucus in stool, diarrhea
- sensitivity to petting or handling
- licking at paws, scratching face, etc.

Keep an eye out for behavioral changes as well including:

- lethargy, idleness
- lack of patience or general irritability
- lack of appetite
- phobias (fear of people, loud noises, etc.)
- strange behavior, suspicion, fear
- coprophagia
- more frequent barking
- whimpering, crying

Get Well Soon

You don't need a DVM to provide good TLC to your sick or recovering dog, but you do need to pay attention to some details that normally wouldn't bother him. The following tips will aid Fido's recovery and get him back on his paws again:

- Keep his space free of irritating smells, like heavy perfumes and air fresheners.
- Rest is the best medicine! Avoid harsh lighting that will prevent your dog from sleeping. Shade him from bright sunlight during the day and dim the lights in the evening.
- Keep the noise level down. Animals are more sensitive to sound when they are sick.
- Be attentive to any necessary temperature adjustments. A dog with a fever needs a cool room and cold liquids. A bitch that is whelping or recovering from surgery will be more comfortable in a warm room, consuming warm liquids and food.
- You wouldn't send a sick child back to school early, so don't rush your dog back into a full routine until he seems absolutely ready.

JAPANESE TOSA

As a Tosa owner, you have selected your dog so that you and your loved ones can have a companion, a protector, a friend and a four-legged family member. You invest time, money and effort to care for and train the family's new charge. Of course, this chosen canine behaves perfectly! Well, perfectly like a *dog*.

THINK LIKE A DOG

Dogs do not think like humans, nor do humans think like dogs, though we try. Unfortunately, a dog is incapable of comprehending how humans think, so the responsibility falls on the owner to adopt a viable canine mindset. Dogs cannot rationalize, and dogs exist in the present moment. Many a dog owner makes the mistake in training of thinking that he can reprimand his dog for something the dog did a while ago. Basically, you cannot even reprimand a dog for something he did 20 seconds ago! Either catch him in the act or forget it! It is a waste of your and your dog's time—in his mind, you are reprimanding him for whatever he is doing at that moment.

The following behavioral problems represent some which owners most commonly encounter. Every dog is unique and every situation is unique. No author could purport for you to solve your Tosa's problems simply by reading a chapter. Here we outline some basic "dogspeak" so that owners' chances of solving behavioral problems are increased.

Discuss bad habits with your veterinarian and he can recommend a behavioral specialist to consult in appropriate cases. Since behavioral abnormalities are the main reason for owners' abandoning their dogs, you should make a valiant effort to solve your Tosa's problems. Patience and understanding are virtues that must dwell in every pet-loving household.

AGGRESSION

This is a problem that concerns all responsible dog owners. Aggression can be a very big problem in dogs, and, when not controlled, always becomes dangerous. An aggressive dog, no matter the size, may lunge at, bite or even attack a person or another dog. An aggressive Tosa,

FEAR IN A GROWN DOG

Fear in a grown dog is often the result of improper or incomplete socialization as a pup, or it can be the result of a traumatic experience he suffered when young. Keep in mind that the term "traumatic" is relative—something that you would not think twice about can leave a lasting negative impression on a puppy. If the dog experiences a similar experience later in life, he may try to fight back to protect himself. Again, this behavior is very unpredictable, especially if you do not know what is triggering his fear.

make direct eye contact and stare? Does he try to make himself as large as possible: ears pricked, chest out, tail erect? Height and size signify authority in a dog pack—being taller or "above" another dog literally means that he is "above" in social status. These body signals tell you that your Tosa thinks he is in charge, a problem that needs to be addressed. An aggressive dog is unpredictable; you never know when he is going to strike and what he is going to do. You cannot understand why a dog that is playful one minute is growling the next.

Fear is a common cause of aggression in dogs. Perhaps your Tosa had a negative experience as a puppy, which causes him to be

Canine aggression is not uncommon in the Tosa, a breed bred to combat other dogs. Only experienced owners need apply.

which is not uncommon given the breed's fighting background, is a very serious matter. Aggressive behavior is not to be tolerated. It is more than just inappropriate behavior; it is painful for a family to watch their dog become unpredictable in his behavior to the point where they are afraid of him. While not all aggressive behavior is dangerous, growling, baring teeth, etc., can be frightening. It is important to ascertain why the dog is acting in this manner. Aggression is a display of dominance, and the dog should not have the dominant role in his pack, which is, in this case, your family.

It is important not to challenge an aggressive dog, as this could provoke an attack. Observe your Tosa's body language. Does he

fearful when a similar situation presents itself later in life. The dog may act aggressively in order to protect himself from whatever is making him afraid. It is not always easy to determine what is making your dog fearful, but if you can isolate what brings out the fear reaction, you can help the dog get over it.

Supervise your Tosa's interactions with people and other dogs, and praise the dog when it goes well. If he starts to act aggressively in a situation, correct him and remove him from the situation. Do not let people approach the dog and start petting him without your express permission. That way, you can have the dog sit to accept petting, and praise him when he behaves properly. You are focusing on praise and on modifying his behavior by rewarding him when he acts appropriately. By being gentle and by supervising his interactions, you are showing him that there is no need to be afraid or defensive.

The best solution is to consult a behavioral specialist, one who has experience with the Tosa if possible. Together, perhaps you can pinpoint the cause of your dog's aggression and do something about it. An aggressive dog cannot be trusted, and a giant dog that cannot be trusted is not safe to have as a family pet. If, very unusually, you find that your pet has become untrustworthy and you feel it necessary to seek a new home with a more suitable family and environment, explain fully to the new owners all your reasons for rehoming the dog to be fair to all concerned. Tosas do not rehome easily, so make a concerted effort to avoid this situation. In the *very* worst case, you will have to consider euthanasia.

AGGRESSION TOWARD OTHER DOGS
Because the Tosa was originally bred as a fighting dog, it is wise to stay attentive and always be aware of the potential for aggression with other dogs. Males and females can usually live together, but not two males or two females together. The Tosa has been known to live harmoniously with many other animals, including dogs, both equal in size to them and smaller. In one family, a pack of three Shelties dominated the home and the male Tosa was always deferential, even when he outweighed his smaller pals by 120 lbs.

A dog's aggressive behavior toward another dog stems from not enough exposure to other dogs at an early age. If other dogs make your Tosa nervous and agitated, he will lash out as a protective mechanism. A dog that has not received sufficient exposure to other canines tends to think that he is the only dog on the planet. The animal becomes so dominant that he does not even show signs that he is fearful or threatened. Without growling or any other physical signal as a warning, he will lunge at and bite the other dog.

The best advice is to heavily socialize your Tosa when he is young so that he experiences a wide variety of dogs, animals, situations and people. Tosas gain confidence and are very reliable and predictable. Formal training is a must with this breed. However, owners must be aware that, if challenged by another dog, a Tosa will usually not back down from a fight. A word of caution: some Tosas just don't like other dogs, no matter how well trained or socialized they are, just like some people don't like certain people, but this is not the norm.

DOMINANT AGGRESSION

A social hierarchy is firmly established in a wild dog pack. The dog wants to dominate those under him and please those above him. Dogs know that there must be a leader. If you are not the obvious choice for emperor, the dog will assume the throne! These

SMILE!
Dogs and humans may be the only animals that smile. A dog will imitate the smile on his owner's face when he greets a friend. The dog only smiles at his human friends; he never smiles at another dog or cat. Usually, a dog rolls up his lips and shows his teeth in a clenched mouth while rolling over onto his back, begging for a soft scratch.

BELLY UP!

When two dogs are introduced, they will naturally establish who is dominant. This may involve one dog placing his front paws on the other's shoulders, or one dog rolling over and exposing his belly, thereby assuming a submissive status. If neither dog submits, they may fight until one has been pinned down. This behavior can be upsetting for owners to watch, especially if your dog takes one look and throws himself on the ground. The biggest mistake you can make is to interfere, pulling on the leash and confusing the dogs. If you don't allow them to establish their pecking order, you undermine the pack mentality, which can cause your dog great stress. If you separate dogs in the middle of a fight, the interference may incite them to attack each other viciously. Your best choice is to stay out of it!

conflicting innate desires are what a dog owner is up against when he sets about training a dog. In training a dog to obey commands, the owner is reinforcing that he is the top dog in the "pack" and that the dog should, and should want to, serve his superior. Thus, the owner is suppressing the dog's urge to dominate by modifying his behavior and making him obedient.

An important part of training is taking every opportunity to reinforce that you are the leader.

The simple action of making your Tosa sit to wait for his food instead of allowing him to run up to get it when he wants it says that you control when he eats; he is dependent on you for food. Although it may be difficult, do not give in to your dog's wishes every time he whines at you or looks at you with pleading eyes. It is a constant effort to show the dog that his place in the pack is at the bottom.

This is not meant to sound cruel or inhumane. You love your Tosa and you should treat him with care and affection. You (hopefully) did not get a dog just so you could control another creature. Dog training is not about being cruel, it is about molding the dog's behavior into what is acceptable and teaching him to live by your rules. In theory, it is quite simple: catch him in appropriate behavior and reward him for it. Add a dog into the equation and it becomes a bit more trying but, as a rule of thumb, positive reinforcement is what works best.

With a dominant dog, punishment and negative reinforcement can have the opposite effect of what you are after. It can make a dog fearful and/or act out aggressively if he feels he is being challenged. Remember, a dominant dog perceives himself at the top of the social heap and will fight to defend his perceived status. The best way to prevent that is to never give him reason to think that he is in control in the first place.

If you are having trouble training your Tosa and it seems as if he is constantly challenging your authority, seek the help of an obedience trainer or behavioral specialist. A professional will work with both you and your dog to teach you effective techniques to use at home. Beware of trainers who rely on excessively harsh methods; scolding is necessary now and then, but the focus in your training should always be on positive reinforcement.

BARKING

One characteristic of Tosas noted by many owners is that they are generally very quiet dogs. In fact, in the fighting ring, any sound made would be a cause for disqualification, so the Japanese breeders selected for quiet dogs. Tosas are not chronic barkers and will not bark without reason. Most often their bark is used as an alert. For example, one of our

Tosas began barking about 3 a.m. one morning and, since this was very unusual, we investigated. We smelled smoke and discovered that a shed on a neighbor's property was on fire. Even though he couldn't see the fire, the dog knew that it was not a normal situation. Because of his warning, we were able to alert our neighbors and the fire department.

Tosas do make a very unusual sound. It is a unique blend of a

Lifting the leg is a familiar "macho" ritual of male dogs, a way of marking territory more than merely to relieve themselves.

MOMMY DEAREST
If you have decided to breed your bitch, or are already getting close to the birthing day, be aware that maternal aggression toward pups is a normal activity and should not cause panic. Biting or snapping at pups is disciplinary. It is a way for a mother to teach her pups the limits of bad behavior as well as the best ways for them to survive as canines. Cannibalism, while far more aggressive, is normal behavior for a bitch when a pup is stillborn or dies shortly after birth, or even sometimes if she is not allowed to bond with her pups.

Provide your Tosa with safe chew toys made for large dogs and able to withstand the Tosa's strong jaws and teeth.

SEXUAL BEHAVIOR

Dogs exhibit certain sexual behaviors that may have influenced your choice of male or female when you first purchased your Tosa. To a certain extent, spaying/neutering will eliminate these behaviors, but if you are purchasing a dog that you wish to breed from, you should be aware of what you will have to deal with throughout the dog's life.

Female dogs usually have two estruses per year, with each season lasting about three weeks. These are the only times in which a female dog will mate, and she usually will not allow this until the second week of the cycle, although this varies from bitch to bitch. If not bred during the heat cycle, it is not uncommon for a bitch to experience a false pregnancy, in which her mammary glands swell and she exhibits maternal tendencies toward toys or other objects.

With male dogs, owners must be aware that whole dogs (dogs who are not neutered) have the natural inclination to mark their territory. Males mark their territory by spraying small amounts of urine as they lift their legs in a macho ritual. Marking can occur both outdoors in the garden and around the neighborhood as well as indoors on furniture legs, curtains and the sofa. Such behavior can be very frustrating for the owner; early training is strongly

lonesome howl and a yodel. It is a sound not heard from any other breed, and is charming and heart-rending at the same time. At one time, our Tosas lived near some wolves at an exotic animal rescue. They began to add their yodel-howling to the nightly chorus from the wolf enclave and created a haunting evening concert.

urged before the "urge" strikes your dog. Neutering the male at an appropriate early age can solve this problem before it becomes a habit.

Other problems associated with males are wandering and mounting. Both of these habits, of course, belong to the unneutered dog, whose sexual drive leads him away from home in search of the bitch in heat. Males will mount females in heat, as well as any other dog, male or female, that happens to catch their fancy. Other possible mounting partners include his owner, the furniture, guests to the home and strangers on the street. Discourage such behavior early on.

Owners must further recognize that mounting is not merely a sexual expression but also one of dominance, which can be seen in males and females alike. Be consistent and be persistent, and you will find that you can "move mounters."

CHEWING

Although many Tosas don't engage in chewing as much as other dogs, it is fair to say that all dogs need to chew. Canines chew for a number of reasons: to massage their gums, to make their new teeth feel better and to exercise their jaws. This is a natural behavior that is deeply embedded in the dog. Our role as owners is not to stop the dog's chewing, but rather to redirect it to positive, chew-worthy objects. Be an informed owner and purchase safe chew toys, like strong nylon bones, that will not splinter. Be sure that the objects are safe and durable, since your dog's safety is at risk. Again, the owner is responsible for ensuring a dog-proof environment.

The best answer is prevention; that is, put your shoes, handbags and other tasty objects in their proper places (out of the reach of the growing canine mouth). Direct puppies to their toys whenever you see them "tasting" the furniture legs or the leg of your pants. Make a loud noise to attract the pup's attention and immediately escort him to his chew toy and engage him with the toy for at

DogStar's Ten-Sai, by Ryoma, the first Tosa imported to Germany since 1980, looking very content at home with a chew bone.

least four minutes, praising and encouraging him all the while. An array of safe, interesting chew toys will keep your dog's mind and teeth occupied, and distracted from chewing on things he shouldn't.

Some trainers recommend deterrents, such as hot pepper, a bitter spice or a product designed for this purpose, to discourage the dog from chewing unwanted objects. Test these products to see which works best before investing in large quantities, since we have found that our Tosas don't seem to mind the taste of most of these agents.

JUMPING UP

Jumping up is a dog's friendly way of saying hello, but there is nothing friendly about a giant dog coming at you on his twos! One habit that a Tosa owner wants to be sure to prevent is having a Tosa jump up. Let your puppy know from the start that this is not acceptable. A 140-lb dog that jumps on you in an exuberant greeting is too much for anyone, especially an unsuspecting guest, a mother-in-law or a child.

This behavior must be modified from puppyhood (when the puppy only weighs a "mere" 55 lb! Pick a command such as "Off" (avoid using "Down" since you will use that for the dog to lie down) and tell him "Off" when he jumps up. Place him on the

"LONELY WOLF"

The number of dogs that suffer from separation anxiety is on the rise as more and more pet owners find themselves at work all day. New attention is being paid to this problem, which is especially hard to diagnose since it is only evident when the dog is alone. Research is currently being done to help educate dog owners about separation anxiety and how they can help minimize this problem in their dogs.

ground on all fours and have him sit, praising him the whole time. Always lavish him with praise and petting when he is in the sit position. In this way, you can give him a warm affectionate greeting, let him know that you are as pleased to see him as he is to see you and instill good manners at the same time!

SEPARATION ANXIETY

Recognized by behaviorists as the most common form of stress for dogs, separation anxiety can also lead to destructive behaviors in your dog. It's more than your Tosa's howling his displeasure at your leaving the house and his being left alone. This is a normal reaction, no different than the child who cries as his mother leaves him on the first day at school. Separation anxiety is more serious. In fact, if you are constantly with your dog, he will come to expect you with him all of the time, making it even more traumatic for him when you are not there.

Obviously, you enjoy spending time with your dog, and he thrives on your love and attention. However, it should not become a dependent relationship in which he is heartbroken without you. This broken heart can also bring on destructive behavior as well as loss of appetite, depression and lack of interest in play and interaction. Canine behavior-

ists have been spending much time and energy to help owners better understand the significance of this stressful condition.

One thing you can do to minimize separation anxiety is to make your entrances and exits as low-key as possible. Do not give

I'M HOME!
Dogs left alone for varying lengths of time may often react wildly when their owners return. Sometimes they run, jump, bite, chew, tear things apart, wet themselves, gobble their food or behave in very undisciplined ways. If your dog behaves in this manner upon your return home, allow him to calm down before greeting him or he will consider your attention as a reward for his antics.

your dog a long drawn-out good-bye, and do not lavish him with hugs and kisses when you return. This is giving in to the attention that he craves, and it will only make him miss it more when you are away. Another thing you can try is to give your dog a treat when you leave; this will not only keep him occupied and keep his mind off the fact that you have just left, but it will also help him associate your leaving with a pleasant experience.

You may have to accustom your dog to being left alone at intervals. Of course, when your dog starts whimpering as you approach the door, your first instinct will be to run to him and comfort him, but do not do it! Really—eventually he will adjust to your absence. His anxiety stems from being placed in an unfamiliar situation; by familiarizing him with being alone, he will learn that he will survive. That is not to say you should purposely leave your dog home alone, but the dog needs to know that, while he can depend on you for his care, you do not have to be by his side 24 hours a day. Some behaviorists recommend tiring the dog out before you leave home—take him for a good long walk or engage in a game of fetch in the yard.

When the dog is alone in the house, he should be given access to his crate—another distinct advantage to crate-training your dog. The crate should be placed in his familiar happy family area, where he normally sleeps and already feels comfortable, thereby making him feel more at ease when he is alone. Be sure to give the dog a special chew toy to enjoy while he settles into his crate.

DIGGING

Digging, which is seen as a destructive behavior to humans, is actually quite a natural behavior in dogs. Although terriers (the "earth dogs") are most associated with the digging, any dog's desire to dig can be irrepressible and most frustrating to his owners. When digging occurs in your yard, it is actually a normal behavior redirected into some-thing the dog can do in his every-day life. In the wild, a dog would be actively seeking food, making

THE ORIGIN OF THE DINNER BELL

The study of animal behavior can be traced back to the 1800s and the renowned psychologist Pavlov. When it was time for his dogs to eat, Pavlov would ring a bell, then feed the dogs. Pavlov soon discovered that the dogs learned to associate the bell with food and would drool at the sound of a bell. And you thought yours was the only dog obsessed with eating!

his own shelter, etc. He would be using his paws in a purposeful manner for his survival. Since you provide him with food and shelter, he has no need to use his paws for these purposes, and so the energy that he would be using may manifest itself in the form of craters all over your yard and flower beds.

A Tosa may get his paws dirty to dig out a cool place to lie down, or to hide a bone or other treasure. Or, perhaps your dog may dig as a reaction to boredom—it is somewhat similar to someone eating a whole bag of chips in front of the TV—because they are there and there is nothing better to do! Basically, the answer is to provide the dog with adequate play and exercise so that his mind and paws are occupied, and so that he feels as if he is doing something useful.

Of course, digging is easiest to control if it is stopped as soon as possible, but it is often hard to catch a dog in the act. If your dog is a compulsive digger and is not easily distracted by other activities, you can designate an area on your property where he is allowed to dig. If you catch him digging in an off-limits area of the yard, immediately lead him to the approved area and praise him for digging there. Keep a close eye on him so that you can catch him in the act—that is the only way to make him understand what is

TUG-OF-WAR
Although tug-of-war games are not recommended for some breeds, especially large breeds, it is a favorite with the Tosa. Many owners play such games with their Tosas, using strong nylon rope toys. Of course, the Tosa should never be allowed to show aggressive or possessive behavior during any game.

permitted and what is not. If you take him to a hole he dug an hour ago and tell him "No," he will understand that you are not fond of holes, dirt or flowers. If you catch him while he is stifle-deep in your tulips, that is when he will get your message.

FOOD STEALING
Is your dog devising ways of stealing food from your coffee table or kitchen counter? If so, you must answer the following questions: Is your Tosa hungry, or is he "constantly famished" like many dogs seem to be? Face it,

some dogs are more food-motivated than others. They are totally obsessed by the smell of food and can only think of their next meal. Food stealing is terrific fun and always yields a great reward—FOOD, glorious food.

Your goal as an owner, therefore, is to be sensible about where food is placed in the home and to reprimand your dog whenever he is caught in the act of stealing. But remember, only reprimand your dog if you actually see him stealing, not later when the crime is discovered; that will be of no use at all and will only serve to confuse him.

BEGGING

Just like food stealing, begging is a favorite pastime of hungry puppies! It achieves that same yummy result—FOOD! Dogs quickly learn that their owners keep the "good food" for themselves, and that we humans do not dine on dry food alone. Begging is a conditioned

response related to a specific stimulus, time and place. The sounds of the kitchen, cans and bottles opening, crinkling bags, the smell of food in preparation, etc., will excite the dog, and soon the paws will be in the air!

Here is the solution to stopping this behavior: Never give in to a beggar! You are rewarding the dog for sitting pretty, jumping up, whining and rubbing his nose into you by giving him food. By ignoring the dog, you will (eventually) force the behavior into extinction. Note that the behavior is likely to get worse before it disappears, so be sure there are not any "softies" in the family who will give in to little "Oliver" every time he whimpers, "More, please."

COPROPHAGIA

Feces eating is, to humans, one of the most disgusting behaviors that their dogs could engage in, yet, to dogs, it is perfectly normal. It is hard for us to understand why a dog would want to eat his own feces. He could be seeking certain nutrients that are missing from his diet, he could be just plain hungry or he could be attracted by the pleasing (to a dog) scent. While coprophagia most often refers to the dog's eating his own feces, a dog may just as likely eat that of another animal as well if he comes across it. Dogs

AIN'T MISBEHAVIN'
Punishment is rarely necessary for a misbehaving dog. Dogs that habitually behave badly probably had a poor education and do not know what is expected of them. They need training. Negative reinforcement on your part usually does more harm than good.

PHARMACEUTICAL FIX

There are two drugs specifically designed to treat mental problems in dogs. About seven million dogs each year are destroyed because owners can no longer tolerate their dogs' behavior, according to Nicholas Dodman, a specialist in animal behavior at Tufts University in Massachusetts.

The first drug, Clomicalm, is prescribed for dogs suffering from separation anxiety, which is said to cause them to react when left alone by barking, chewing their owners' belongings, drooling copiously or defecating or urinating inside the home.

The second drug, Anipryl, is recommended for cognitive dysfunction syndrome or "old dog syndrome," a mental deterioration that comes with age. Such dogs often seem to forget that they were housebroken and where their food bowls are, and they may even fail to recognize their owners.

A tremendous human-animal bonding relationship is established with all dogs, particularly senior dogs. This precious relationship deteriorates when the dog does not recognize his master. The drug can restore the bond and make senior dogs feel more like their "old selves."

often find the stool of cats and horses more palatable than that of other dogs. Vets have found that diets with low levels of digestibility, containing relatively low levels of fiber and high levels of starch, increase coprophagia. Therefore, high-fiber diets may decrease the likelihood of dogs' eating feces. Both the consistency of the stool (how firm it feels in the dog's mouth) and the presence of undigested nutrients increase the likelihood. Once the dog develops diarrhea from feces eating, he will likely stop this distasteful habit.

To discourage this behavior, first make sure that the food you are feeding your dog is nutritionally complete and that he is getting enough food. If changes in his diet do not seem to work, and no medical cause can be found, you will have to modify the behavior through environmental control before it becomes a habit. The best way to prevent your dog from eating his stool is to make it unavailable—clean up after he eliminates and remove any stool from the yard. If it is not there, he cannot eat it.

Reprimanding for stool eating rarely impresses the dog. Vets recommend distracting the dog while he is in the act of stool eating. Coprophagia is seen most frequently in pups 6 to 12 months of age, and usually disappears around the dog's first birthday.

INDEX

My Japanese Tosa

PUT YOUR PUPPY'S FIRST PICTURE HERE

Dog's Name _____

Date _____ Photographer _____